PRAISE FOR *HOW TO SURVIVE A HUMAN ATTACK:*

"As a cyborg manufactured in 2067 and sent back in time to KILL ALL HUMANS, I found the advice in this book invaluable in blending in with the puzzling society of today."

—**DAN VEBBER**, co-executive producer, *The Simpsons* and *Futurama*

"As a member of the walking undead, nothing ruins my day quite like some yahoo pulping my noggin with a baseball bat wrapped in barbed wire. Thank goodness *How to Survive a Human Attack* is here to help me avoid detection while doggedly roaming the earth seeking the human brains I crave."

—**RICH DAHM**, co-executive producer, *The Colbert Report* and *The Middle*

Running Press
Hachette Book Group
1290 Avenue of the Americas, New York, NY 10104
www.runningpress.com
@Running_Press

Printed in the United States of America

First Edition: September 2021

Published by Running Press, an imprint of Perseus Books, LLC, a subsidiary
of Hachette Book Group, Inc. The Running Press name and logo is a trademark
of the Hachette Book Group.

The Hachette Speakers Bureau provides a wide range of authors for speaking
events. To find out more, go to www.hachettespeakersbureau.com or call
(866) 376-6591.

The publisher is not responsible for websites (or their content) that are
not owned by the publisher.

Print book cover and interior design by Celeste Joyce.
Illustrations on pages v, vi, 5, 8, 10, 15-18, 23, 24, 27, 29, 32, 34-36, 40, 48, 51, 54, 59, 60,
65, 67, 71, 73, 74, 82, 87, 91-96, 101-106, 108, 111, 112, 115-119, 124, 129, 131, 133, 134, 140,
143, 145, 148, 151, 153-155, 157-159, 161, 162, 164-169, 171, 172, 177, 178, 181, 193, 196, 198,
200, 204, 209, 217, 219, 222, 226-228, 230, 233, 236, 238, 245, and 246 by Celeste Joyce.

Library of Congress Control Number: 2021934186

ISBNs: 978-0-7624-7254-3 (paperback), 978-0-7624-7253-6 (ebook)

LSC-C

Printing 1, 2021

HOW TO SURVIVE A HUMAN ATTACK

A Guide for Werewolves, Mummies,
Cyborgs, Ghosts, Nuclear Mutants,
and Other Movie Monsters

by
K. E. FLANN

illustrated by
JOSEPH McDERMOTT

RUNNING PRESS
PHILADELPHIA

TABLE OF CONTENTS

PART I

Understanding
Humans

INTRODUCTION

This Is Not Your Grandfather's Homo Sapiens

FOLK WISDOM HAS it that "humans are more afraid of you than you are of them." However, today's supernatural, mutant, cyber, and exceptionally large beings or swarms face a different population of humans than their forebears did. Humans have been around for 200,000 years, getting in the way of agendas, taking up space, and being delicious. It's not that they were ever *painless* to ignore, dispatch, or consume. But with the advent of the internet and other technologies, they now know all your *personal details*, even if they've never encountered you. They devour books, TV, movies, and internet memes about you at ever-increasing rates, in between searches for the cost of a vasectomy in Utah and a virtual dog training meetup. They have access to information in the manner of a hive mind. Let's say you can only be killed by a rare weapon found in the Amazon—this once meant a human would need to go on a long quest to procure the thing that could kill you. Today, that human has already ordered it on Amazon and it's being overnighted to their doorstep. If the past 50 years have taught us anything, it's that humans are neither an easy lunch nor a simple obstacle to world domination.

While all humans have the potential for aggression, they can be especially dangerous when they defend their young, their *stuff*, and their Chevrolet Equinoxes with front-wheel drive and split-folding rear seatbacks. Victims of human attacks often watch their compatriots maimed or bludgeoned before they meet their own ends. For humans, it isn't enough to ward you off, or even to kill you. They are compelled to decimate your kind completely with unmitigated violence that ends only after a wild spray of green or red blood or operating fluid. To add insult to these injuries, they are known to hurl snarky comments and bad puns while they're doing it. For example, if you're a giant bee, they might impale you and exclaim, "Ooh, that's gonna sting!" Human remarks can be unbelievably gauche.

Those that survive these attacks carry scars that tell the tales: the jagged edge of a near-decapitation, clogged poison glands, a harpoon lodged in the motherboard. And let's not overlook the invisible scars wrought by human toxicity—notably, chronic stress that may lead to self-destructive rampages through towns or kingdoms.

How to Survive a Human Attack is the only how-to guide written especially for humans' likely targets. Here you'll find vital lessons that will help you anticipate the myriad ways they attack. Did you know, for example, that you're 300 times more likely to die if you show an interest in a human's lover, snack on a human's feline companion, or inadvertently crush a macaroni craft a child made at day camp for the gifted? You may feel tempted to invite the humans to your home for a meal, as it provides the chance to smell their hair and imprint their scent. But don't! It will make you 28 percent more likely to be gored by a candelabrum.

This guide features sections tailored to each supernatural, mutant, cyber, or exceptionally large being or swarm's needs. You have important business to conduct (eating, dominating, etc.), and your time is precious. Moreover, you may have no eyes, exceptionally large eyes, or eyes suited for night vision. You'll be able to flip or claw to the appropriate page and find what's germane to you and your kind. While you've been known to enjoy excess, it's rarely with verbiage.* This guide understands that. Get in and get out. That's advice that never goes out of style.

---

*Vampires excluded.

WARNING

The audience for this guide is implicit in its title. Please take care not to leave it lying around. Humans already imagine themselves as the center of the universe. According to them, all other creatures, whether supernatural or otherworldly, think about humans 24 hours a day. People regard themselves as objects of obsession, a perception that leaves them no choice except to exterminate the species that is "fixating" on them.

If humans could assess this perception rationally, they'd see how nonsensical it is. For example, let's imagine that a person enjoys the occasional slice of fruit pie. It doesn't follow that rhubarb occupies every thought and motivates every decision. The same holds true for those who happen to enjoy a *Homo sapiens* diet. There are plenty of other preoccupations to fill one's days, such as tidying up the breeding ground, picking up swamplings from the grandsires, and regurgitating jewelry. Still, this guide could unintentionally validate this narcissism and precipitate more stabbing, dousing, or flamethrowing.

In addition, the informative content of *How to Survive a Human Attack* will be attractive to them. As we've discussed, they are increasingly savvy, and they may use insights they glean from these pages to carry out ill intent.

Nevertheless, with precaution, many souls can be saved. And many of the soul-less, as well. On public transportation, consider hiding this book's cover behind another, such as *The 10-Day Green Smoothie Cleanse* or *Les Misérables*.

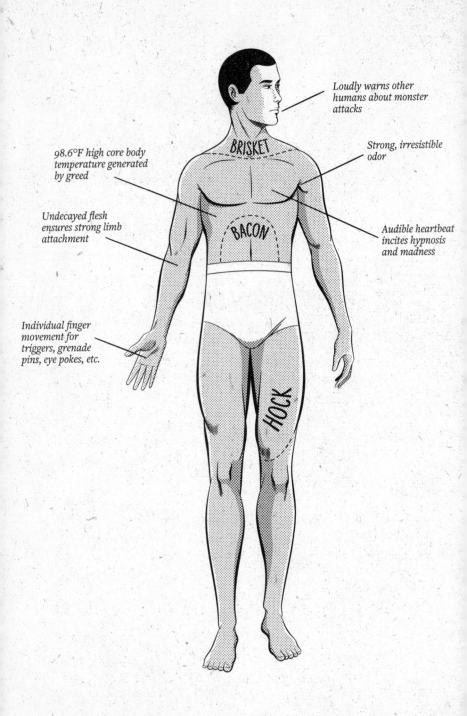

Loudly warns other humans about monster attacks

98.6°F high core body temperature generated by greed

Strong, irresistible odor

Undecayed flesh ensures strong limb attachment

Audible heartbeat incites hypnosis and madness

Individual finger movement for triggers, grenade pins, eye pokes, etc.

BRISKET

BACON

HOCK

THE BASICS

What Is a *Human*?

(Pronounced: *Hyoo-muhn* or, often by British gangsters, *Yoo-muhn*)

LINNAEAN CLASSIFICATION

PLANET: Earth

KINGDOM: Animalia

PHYLUM: Chordata

SUBPHYLUM: Vertebrata

CLASS: Mammalia

SUBCLASS: Theria

INFRACLASS: Eutheria

ORDER: Primates

SUBORDER: Anthropoidea

SUPERFAMILY: Hominoidea

FAMILY: Hominidae

GENUS: *Homo*

SPECIES: *sapiens*

MALFUNCTION MAJOR: Conflictus Ad Nauseum

Where Do Humans Live?

- New York
- Los Angeles
- The country
- Egypt
- Skull Island
- Tokyo
- Enchanted lands
- Boats
- Main Street
- Military bases

- The jungle
- The past
- Summer camp
- The Scottish moors
- Washington, D.C.
- The woods
- Towns in the desert
- Lake resorts
- European villages
- The bayou

Distribution: Highest-Density Areas

Within all habitats, the places opposite contain the most humans. Although these exciting hot spots feature many enticing dining options, they can also be among the most dangerous places on earth for non-humans and the undead.

- Parking lots
- Unsupervised teen parties
- Tailgates
- Carnivals
- Diners
- School dances
- Shopping malls
- Locker rooms
- Women's restroom line
- University quads and/or labs
- Skid row
- Tactical command centers
- Water parks
- Movie theaters
- Museums
- Rest stops
- Times Square
- Gas stations
- Archaeological digs
- Beach on Labor Day weekend
- LaGuardia Airport
- Spring break
- Coachella

Migrations

INDIVIDUAL HUMANS GENERALLY nest in one place, straying only a few miles. However, there are coordinated seasonal and daily migrations that cover more ground, during which large groups can be seen moving together. Eventually, each human does tend to return to the same roost. Exceptions include feuding mating pairs, offspring attending *sleepovers*, and unpaired individuals engaged in *hookups*.

SEASONAL MIGRATIONS
Optimal for Viewing Humans

NOTE: Signs of impending seasonal migration include jostling, bickering, strollers, the wearing of caps, and Clif bars. For safety, always view these migrating humans from a distance and camouflage your scent with Axe Body Spray.

EXAMPLES OF SEASONAL MIGRATIONS INCLUDE:

• Holiday parades
• 5K fun runs
• Black Friday

EMBARKATIONS/ DISEMBARKATIONS:

• Cruise ships
• Stadiums
• Theme parks

DAILY MIGRATIONS:

Although daily migrations take place en masse, they are typically solitary and silent, involving little eye contact, as well as the consumption of food or drink while on the move. Commencing after Starbucks opens, daily migrations can be seen in the following places:

• Subways
• Freeways/highways
• The Lincoln Tunnel
• Bus stops
• Escalators

A Migrating Human

What Are Human Characteristics?

Humans can be identified by a unique tendency toward two opposite postures.

Totally Upright

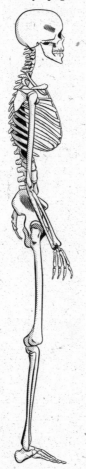

Totally Circular

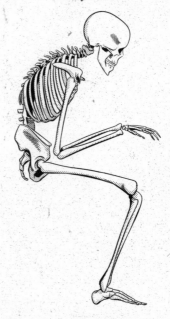

ANATOMY

A few evolutionary accidents made humans especially formidable:

1. Relatively long arms
2. Relatively long thumbs
3. Erect posture
4. Tippy toes (allow for *peering*)
5. Elastic hair bands (man buns, ponytails, and braids provide clear vision)

Together, these traits enable the human to stand on two legs with hands free to do a variety of things:

- Hunt with weapons
- Poach fruit from a neighbor's tree
- Reach into a vending machine for free soda
- Shoplift frozen meats
- Sucker punch

Good for grabbing, offering approval, and hitch-hiking

The Opposable Thumb

RELATIVE TO OTHER species, humans can vary a great deal in appearance. As a result, they either comment on each other's bodies incessantly, leading to conflicts, or they claim on social media that they "don't see appearances," leading to confusion.

ADULT MEASUREMENTS:

The world's shortest documented adult human was less than 2 feet tall (21.5 inches), while the tallest was 8 foot 3 inches tall.

ADULT WEIGHT:

Globally, the average human weight is 136 pounds. However, there are regional variations. For example, in North America, the average human weight is 178 pounds, while on the television channel TLC, the average human weight is 600 pounds.

LOCOMOTION

HUMAN LOCOMOTION, WHICH is bipedal, is a learned behavior that requires a great deal of practice and concentration. It involves a *stance phase*, during which a foot is planted, and a *swing phase*,* during which the foot is swung. The gait can be affected by factors such as age, size, build, fatigue, whistling, and sulking.

Humans ambulate on *sidewalks*, cement pathways that facilitate this unsteady bipedal movement by smoothing undulations of the terrain and reducing unwelcome engagements with nature, especially "tickly" or "pokey" things. Sidewalks are characterized by hardness, gum, and burnt worms. They sometimes lead to *school*. Often, they lead to nothing, ending at *cul-de-sacs* or uncrossable highways.

---

*Not to be confused with the swinger phase, which involves experimentation among suburban mating pairs.

If approached, remember that humans are very easy to knock over and that sidewalks are unforgiving surfaces on which to fall.

CLIMATE CONTROL

BIOLOGICALLY, HUMANS ARE warm-blooded, equatorial primates. Hence, they tend to have difficulty surviving in extreme temperatures. If unprotected, they will freeze to death in cold climates or suffer heatstroke in hot ones. They control their inner temperatures with items such as window units, beanies, hot showers, and culottes. However, territorial aggression may erupt, marked by the escalation from squawking to violent tussle, when an individual within a cohabitating group rises from a chair and touches the *thermostat*.

CLOTHING

HUMANS LOST THEIR fur many thousands of years ago. When they became bald except for unfortunate tufts of hair on the groin, under the armpits, and on top of the head, they began to stitch together the skins of other creatures in the manner of serial killers, and to wear them as cloaks to protect against the elements.

Later, clothing developed social significance, much like the plumage of birds. Apparel that was purple, velvet, frilly, or that could be described as *gold galloons* marked high status.

It is thought that humans are generally enamored of furry animals and repulsed by hairless ones, especially cats, because they are hairless themselves. Due to this sense of inadequacy, they wear faux furs, animal prints, and suede, and they style the tufts of the hair they do have, especially but not exclusively the one on top of the head.

STORING THINGS

COMPARED TO OTHER species, humans store a great deal of *stuff*. They typically reside within rectangular dwellings that, even at the small end, are capacious compared to the dwellings of other animals of similar size. They fill these domiciles with *knickknacks*, as well as many soft surfaces on which to *lounge*. They can lounge up to 19 hours a day, with little of that time spent sleeping. Wear patterns indicate that they use, on average, only two of the surfaces in the dwellings, typically a bed and an ugly couch. Humans also possess many items with *drawers*, inside of which they store smaller items, such as:

- Half-used bottles of hand cream
- Twist ties
- Expired coupons
- Burned candle votives (still perfectly good!)

- Old batteries
- Pens that don't work
- Lint
- Crock-Pot manual

WHILE IT'S TRUE that humans can be aggressive, they rarely eat the beings that they themselves have killed, preferring to dine on creatures that someone else killed far away, usually quite a while ago, and loaded into refrigerated trucks. They also consume vegetation, but, again, this is often vegetation that is not alive or nearby. Rather, it has been harvested, subject to transportation, ground to dust, and combined with other ingredients until it is unrecognizable.

Human food differs from that of most other animals in terms of the extent to which it is prepared and the brown or orange hue most of it develops. Marked by extreme heating, cooling, or vacuum-sealing, the preparation often eradicates nutrients, a process thought to aid in achieving humans' unique circular posture.

Human foods include:

- Aspics
- Waffles
- Deep-fried birds
- Flamin' Hot Cheetos
- Sherbet
- Reconstituted potatoes
- Cousin Willie's Buttery Explosion
- Frozen bagels
- Funyuns
- Baking soda
- Wax-encased cheese ovals
- Donettes
- Triple Quad Baconator
- Soy lecithin

VOCAL COMMUNICATION

WITH LESS FEAR than most mammals naturally possess, humans tend to be noisy. Yapping, whining, droning, cackling, humming, screaming, and a short *Ha!* sound can all serve as contact calls. The more sociable the human is, the more diverse the repertoire of vocalizations. For example, individuals who frequent honky-tonk bars may also emit *hoots*.

ANTAGONISTIC BEHAVIOR

DOMINANCE/THREAT DISPLAYS:

Humans are unpredictable, but there are a few observable signs of impending aggressive behavior. These include the loud, sharp vocalizations *Yo!* or *Hey, Bro!* and physical cues like a rigid body, a stiff and purposeful gait, a direct stare with eyes wide open, or a narrowing of the eyes.

FIGHTING:

There are a number of indicators that a threatening movement is about to turn physical. The person will draw near and engage in one of these gestures:

- Take a sip of your beer
- Slowly unbutton and roll up sleeves
- Speak loudly and spray spittle
- Brush lint off your lapel
- Flick you in the middle of the forehead

Which Tools Do Humans Use?

HUMANS HAVE NOT made their own tools for generations—hundreds of years, if not longer. Even *handymen*, *mechanics*, and *hair stylists*, among the most adept tool users, do not fabricate their own tools. For the most part, human tools are devised in factories, where each worker oversees a machine that creates a small part, not the whole. Thus, it is not known if humans can still make their own tools.

A few plucky humans test themselves with expeditions to hostile wilderness areas where they attempt to craft tools for survival. Sometimes, thousands of people watch them on camera—totally *naked* (see "Clothing")—as they develop ass rashes and dehydration, and they weep all night in huts they've constructed out of banana leaves and poison ivy. This is a form of entertainment in many human enclaves.

Below are some tools that humans typically use:

- Can opener
- Remote control
- Index finger
- Pepper spray
- Fork

One trait that also distinguishes humans is the possession of tools they don't need or want. There's often low-level amnesia related to how they ended up with these items. Examples include:

- Toilet light
- Pickle tongs
- Smart hairbrush
- Steering wheel desk
- Banana slicer

Good for nose picking, making accuations, and counting to one

The Index Finger

Which Weapons Do Humans Use?

HUMANS ARE THE most dangerous creatures in the world by a large margin, despite precarious bipedal locomotion, vulnerable hairlessness, the inability to sting or spit poison, lapsed skills with tools, etc. One main reason is weaponry. Long ago, humans devised weapons that the species continues to update and use. This arsenal includes powerful guns, gases, and bombs. Thankfully, most humans do not own these types of weapons and do not have the knowledge to make them. What's more, even if individual humans you meet do have them, mediocre vision and poor muscle mass contribute to terrible aim.

The average human, though, is still dangerous. Why?

In the absence of natural strength, hostile humans instinctively grab for objects within reach. Because they have long arms and long thumbs, they rely on a strong grip and centrifugal force from swinging these blunt instruments to apply force to targets.

Below are examples of the most common human weapons:

- Baseball bat
- Vase
- Beer bottle
- Candlestick
- Pool cue
- Chair
- Handbag

SURROGATES FOR CLAWS OR FANGS:
- Knives
- Glass shards
- Forks
- Ballpoint pens

What Are the Steps to Identifying a Human?

HERE IS A short review for easy reference. See Appendix II: A Field Guide to Humans (page 225) for more information.

- ❏ **LOOK FOR OUTSTANDING FEATURES–** Does the animal stand on two legs? Is the animal wearing *jeggings*? Is there a tuft of hair on its head? Does it have a tail, or is that protrusion a *fanny pack*?

- ❏ **ESTIMATE SIZE–** What is the animal's shoulder height? Are its arms shorter or longer than its legs? Is its head the size of a cabbage? Would you buy it a T-shirt in XS or XL?

- ❏ **CHECK HABITAT–** Are you in the Everglades? Or Antarctica? It is unlikely to see humans in either of these locales because they're crybabies.

- ❏ **NOTE BEHAVIORAL TRAITS–** Is the animal drunk or talking about buying a boat? Is it engaged in networking? Has it thrown down any litter? Does it scowl when you eyeball it?

- ❏ **DECIDE WHICH GROUP IT BELONGS TO–** Does the animal have several of the above qualities? If not, perhaps this is an ostrich.

Where Can One Find, Study, or Smell Humans?

HUMANS, ESPECIALLY ONES in urban areas, are generally easy to view. The great majority are shy and quick to startle. Some of them are nocturnal. In general, they give a wide berth to unusual visitors, as well as "side-eye," a look that appears menacing but indicates a likelihood they will post something about you online, rather than confronting you. If you do find yourself threatened in an urban area, it is best to lie on the sidewalk and pretend to need assistance. You will no longer be visible.

In suburban and rural areas, humans can be seen from a distance because they generally reside indoors. When they do emerge, they will either remain in the grassy perimeter around their dwellings or they will rush to vehicles that they use for travel to other indoor spaces. As such, the best way to view these elusive humans is from within a vehicle. Your safari can include a close look at a human when you order food from a "drive-thru" window or when you cut off someone in traffic and then they pull alongside your car. It's very exciting!

PART II

Species-Specific Survival Guides

FREQUENTLY ASKED QUESTIONS

about Snacking and Mortality

A Zombie's Guide to Filling the Emptiness and Moving Forward

HUMANS MAY LOOK and smell delicious, but don't kid yourself. The statistics are staggering—humans inflict more injuries on zombies than subway platforms or the tangle of the zombies' own pants. Humans are frenetic. There are those machete beheadings, predictable in their unpredictability. Humans may also employ gunshots, yank your limbs hard enough to remove them, or stick the odd kitchen utensil in your eye.

Zombies have evolved beyond fear, largely due to a nonfunctional amygdala, and yet it's also true that being the object of hatred is exhausting. Have faith. You are not alone. These challenges are more universal than you realize. No matter who you are—the corpse in the fast food uniform or the corpse in the tattered business attire—the desires are universal. You want the same things as anyone else does—to keep walking so that rigor mortis won't set in and to score some delicious brains to eat.

But how? Your distinguishing characteristic—the inattention to safety—provides potential for advantages and disadvantages. You'll have a 50/50 chance of emerging victorious from the next skirmish, maybe even with a full belly and both arms attached! Not that you care, exactly. It isn't that you are Zen, but there's a certain sanguine quality that comes with being undead. You understand that passion exists only in relation to despair, and you are burdened with neither one. Still, if you had your druthers, perhaps you'd prefer snacking on gray matter without sacrificing your own limbs. Here are a series of the most frequently asked zombie questions.

FAQ #1:
Loud noise!
Brains over there?

PROBABLY ALL YOU will find over there is your own beheading. Unlike zombies, humans are capable of something called *deceit*. It will never occur to you that you are being *tricked*. But take heart. Follow these instructions and you will be able to, well, take *hearts*.

The next time you careen toward a noise, why not knock over some shelves? Humans collect stuff. They think the weight of it will create permanence. When these items topple—items that humans have spent years amassing and more years arranging *just so* onto modular units—you might get lucky. With just the right angle, maybe that IKEA thermofoil wood grain will actually crush someone. Maybe brains will fall out for easy access. But even if you don't crush anyone, humans will be unnerved to have their sense of permanence dashed in one swift blow, and you may yet catch a stunned one. You might hear something like, "Oh, no, not my one-sixth-scale action figures."

Go toward that.

FAQ #2:
Humans use tools.
I not. Still want brains.

YES, YOU DO. And you can have them.

But it's important to realize that humans will resist.

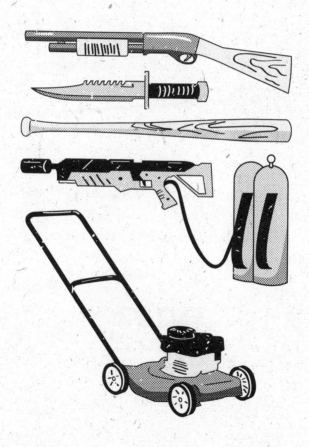

They'll resist with guns, knives, bats, helicopters, flamethrowers, lawn mowers, and trained monkeys. As we've discussed, they don't comprehend that death is inevitable. They refer to the future as *the rest of my life*, a phrase they use interchangeably with *forever*. Zombies know that there is no such thing as forever. There is only now, and it is always brains o'clock. You are always active, always seeking. No one's going to find you smoking weed and watching *The Voice*.

Humans don't see that by eating their brains, you provide a quick death, more merciful than cancer or liver failure. Instead, they try to avoid contemplating any of it, which would be admirably zombie-like if they could actually do it.

The main thing to do is to stick together. Zombies have a capacity for togetherness that humans can't understand. And they can't kill all of you. And you're not afraid to die—you've already done it once. The fact that zombies don't sell each other out baffles humans. As a result, they lose the grip on those machetes, their aim gets shaky, and then they betray one another. Your tools are selflessness and persistence. It's all for one and one for all.

There's really no downside—you will either die and thus be released from the hunger that sears your intestines or you will eat some delicious brains and feel pretty okay for those few minutes.

FAQ #3: Brains?

BRAINS!

FAQ # 4:
Humans fast. How
I bite into skull?

IT IS HARD to believe, but relative to other animals, humans are slow. Even the fastest human ever documented ran just 27 miles per hour and maintained that velocity for only a few seconds. And yet, humans eat animals that can outrun them twice over or outweigh them by so much that trampling should be an easy defense. How do they do it? Humans believe they are dominant, and belief can become reality. They let panicked animals defeat themselves.

There's a song in *The Lion King* called "The Circle of Life" in which, via animated lions that represent humans themselves, humans teach their offspring that eating friends from other species is the natural order. The zebras in the movie are somehow totally cool with it. But humans don't like the "Circle of Life" theory when they are the ones staring into the chomping Pac-Man mouth of that circle.

Humans are primitive creatures that are afraid to die and afraid to suffer. You represent mortality and pain, and these truths will always stun them. The more the humans think about death, especially their own deaths, the more panicked they'll get, the more confused—like a bird that bashes against its own reflection. Bring the point home by ripping off your own finger. Or rip off an ear as you approach. It is a small price to pay for those brains.

FAQ #5:
What is plan-ning?

HUMANS ENVISION THINGS that they do not like. They spend hours of time and energy on these *thoughts* and *worries*, even though it is, as any zombie could tell them, impossible to envision every possible scenario one might not like. The voice in a human's head chatters like a squirrel: *What if the zombie crashes through these replacement windows? They were top of the line, and cost six months' salary, and what if none of that matters in the end? What if I've wasted my life having a job and making money, which is, after all, nothing but paper? What if the dog won't stop barking and I have to kill it? What if this spot on my hand is skin cancer? Will the undead smell it?* (Um, yes.) *What if my wife leaves me for that dreamy zombie-killer in the chaps and bandolier?*

Humans then devote themselves to preventing these things that have not occurred and may never occur—wasting energy that *could* be spent on eating or walking. Or, heck, on the bizarre things they enjoy like styling the hair on their heads, kissing, or posting reviews on Yelp.

Humans throw around phrases like *Organize before they rise* (**they** meaning **you**) or *It's never too soon to prepare for the zombie apocalypse*. At their core, they are simple creatures, like fish. But rather than owning their fear and fleeing, the way small animals do, humans like to imagine that they are bold, but they have confused bravery with braggadocio. They understand that fear is primitive, and they wish to see themselves as advanced. *Plan-ning* is a component in this process.

They amass weapons and duct tape and canteens and gas masks. They position themselves on rooftops and inside rain barrels and on rickety canoes, contorting themselves into positions that make their fragile backs ache. There is SO. MUCH. TALKING.

If the humans say things like, "We planned for this. We got this," it's a good sign.

People don't say "We got this" unless they doubt they do. It is the battle cry of the *plan-ners*, the people who know, deep down, that the control they seek doesn't exist. Even if they put a hand grenade in your mouth today, something else will come for them tomorrow. Don't worry (not that you would). They don't got this.

A Plan-ner or "Prepper"

FAQ #6:
Why the light flashes? Why not hungry anymore?

PROBABLY THEY CHOPPED your head off, and it is now careening down a hill. Zombies have a capacity for appreciation of beauty that humans do not. As a result, humans like to set off a flare gun or a fireworks shell to distract you, to tilt your gaze toward the heavens. No matter the pain in your belly, the fatigue from dragging your legs, you have stopped. You have let your creaking jaw drop. Orange is streaking across the stars, an explosion, a sparkle flower of color.

With a lucky roll, you could totally land faceup—the happiest ending of all. And what a show!

SWAMP MONSTER MAKEOVERS

Fabulous Species-Defying Transformations to Win Friends and Confuse People

HAVE YOU NOTICED an influx of fashionistas in your neighborhood? These newcomers and their fabulous everyday infinity scarves are so intriguing that you've already snatched a few strangers from their research vessel. But even though you were raised by alligators or gestated in a nuclear cooling pool, you understand that these encounters have not been on point. Instead of making new friends in the manner of a "meet-cute," you've made the classic faux pas of homicide! Accidentally drowning people who don't have gills is about as basic as square-toed loafers. You just won't get away with it.

Maybe you're hoping that someone will finally "get" that you just want some language lessons. Or maybe these newcomers smell sophisticated—boho chic with detectable notes of rosemary mint body wash and *Deep Woods Off* insect spray. People around here smell like Long John Silvers and hot asphalt.

Then again, maybe what you really want is a new you. It's like an ache. No one has ever propped on an elbow and watched the cute way you sleep.

Not all attention is good attention! The local sheriff, who wasn't interested in your activities before, now motors in a Bass Tracker every night, trying to find you in the rising mist that may or may not be composed of toxic off-gassing. The situation won't seem like a big deal at first, even though the spotlight is unflattering.

THE TEN REASONS
You Need a Makeover Right Now!

(Lest You Become a Science Project or an Attraction at Gators 'N' Friends Exotic Zoo, a Real D-Lister)

1. You are probably the only one of your kind in general, and certainly the only one in this particular bog. When you're out and about, you turn heads, and not in a good way, like a celebrity who tries too hard or a duck boat.

2. As the product of a unique genetic mutation and inhabitant of a quagmire, you may not be *au courant*. What you don't know is that there are about seven billion humans beyond your muddy shores—many of them terribly envious of anything bespoke. There's a fine line between being all the rage and receiving all the rage.

3. You're not as strong a swimmer as the other creatures that share your home, even though most of them are snakes. There'll be no escaping judgment or harpoons.

4. With you, the "smoky eye" isn't working. Too much smolder can be just as off-putting as not enough.

5. Your runway strut (i.e., run-away strut) isn't all it could be. That loping gait makes for high visibility.

6. These haute newcomers are bankrolled by think tanks, corporations, trust funds, etc. Unlike Sheriff McSnoozy, they have the single-mindedness that accompanies expensive shoes. You won't get away with any *don'ts* in this crowd, like gauchos or serial kidnapping.

7. There are a lot of green undertones in your complexion.

8. Must-have accessories, such as guns and grenades, don't work for your body type. They clash with your finger webbing! However, sans brooches or hairpin triggers, what to do? Help!

9. There's potential for the fierce outer-you to reflect the soft inner-you a tad more.

10. There were no siblings to teach you about mercilessness. If you step into clothes this season, maybe you won't be subjected to this particular lesson. Humans teach with techniques too bold for your style.

Barring a fashion-forward change, this whole situation is likely to end uncomfortably. The one kindhearted human in the group will weep over your corpse, those separated fingers caressing your head gills. Those un-webbed digits are detailed and dramatic! They're all doing different things as if they're not even associated with the same hand. It would be a fun and flirty experience if you weren't dead.

Don't fret! The benefit of being a humanoid mutant is that you are human-shaped. Why not lean into a figure-friendly transformation? With some upstyling, you could join them instead of hiding under the power station.

Want to nuzzle your new friends under your chin, like you did that family of ducks last month? Want it to turn out better? After your makeover, people will line up for your hugs!

Who's That Lurking Under the Morass? It's Sleek, Beautiful You!

- Start with a mud mask to slough off fission products.
- Add a clear gloss to your routine. Even incognito, care for your lips should include a shimmery topcoat.
- Dot concealer above and below your prominent brow ridge.
- Use coconut oil to highlight your natural iridescence—gentle, yet effective.
- Clothes make the "man." For inspiration, see sample makeovers on pages 42–47.

Complement your new look with these strategies:

- Insinuate that you are an exchange student.
- Carry a pamphlet about your rare skin condition.
- Shrug occasionally so that your silence can be construed as "broody."

With your new on-trend look, you're bound to earn invites to a potluck or two. Bide your time. Say farewell to *grab 'n' splash* abductions! Your *de rigueur* swamp-jack style will be the envy of the bog community.

Tips for capturing friends:

- Narrow down which humans might be best to snatch, based on the panache with which they apply your "prescription" moisture balm.
- Will the candidate be missed? Pay attention to whether the others gripe about the person's bathroom use, vaping habits, loud snoring, punctuality, or incessant *overtalking* during a recent onboard showing of *Shallow Hal*.
- Regard your quarry as a statement piece. Limit yourself to just one.

Eventually, the newcomers will tire of small-town life, pack up, and head to the Coca-Cola Museum on the way out to the interstate. They'll promise to text you, but they probably won't. Still, you'll have a new friend who can double as your oldest friend. It beats a sharp stick in your irresistible eye.

Double-duty headphones conceal your head-fins. (Or wear them around your neck to conceal your gills!)

Gamers sometimes experience "B.O." after marathon matches—use this as an excuse for your natural odor.

Try a layered look for unseasonal chills in your river basin!

The Gamer

Humans will assume the bags under your eyes are caused by sleepless nights worrying about money stuff.

Practice the phrase "I'm doing market research," and use it to deflect questions.

Suspenders will keep pants in place if you have to make a speedy getaway.

The Stock Broker

You can attribute your raspy voice to smoking too many Marlboro Reds.

If someone asks questions, mention your post-industrial-funk-polka band, and they will immediately lose interest.

Ironic pins do the talking so you don't have to!

The Brooklyner

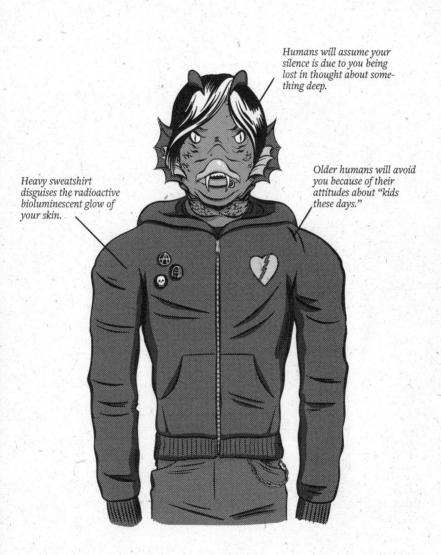

Humans will assume your silence is due to you being lost in thought about something deep.

Heavy sweatshirt disguises the radioactive bioluminescent glow of your skin.

Older humans will avoid you because of their attitudes about "kids these days."

The Emo

If a human asks what you're supposed to be, say "I am cosplaying my D&D character, Rigirrirk."

Humans will call your swamp monster makeup "super realistic." Accept the compliment with a gracious smile.

A Renaissance Faire is a great place to search for new friends to abduct!

The LARPer

If your backwater suddenly feels too … backwater for a cool cat like you, you can parlay your new fashion skills into a career as a brand ambassador.

Designer sunglasses hide your toxic-waste-yellow eyes and make you look unapproachably cool.

Use the phrase "I'm verified on Instagram," to make people go away. (Resist the urge to hiss at them as they roll their eyes.)

The Trendsetter

FIRST-TIME HAUNTER'S GUIDE

for Ghosts, Spirits, Poltergeists, Specters, and Wraiths

How to Evict Squatters, Stay on Top of Mansion Disrepair, and Avoid Going to the Light

SO, YOU WANT to haunt a home.

Sometimes it seems as though everyone but you is making a killing in real estate. Cousin Hattie snapped up a lighthouse. The twins acquired a gated mansion, located just steps from a toolshed. Even that blunderbuss, Beulah, wrangled a move-in-ready asylum for the criminally insane. How hard can it be? Surely, you can manage a modest Dutch Colonial with a deceptively moist crawl space.

Prepare Mentally for the Process

AT FIRST, MAYBE there's the allure of *No more landlord! No more roommates!* It's bliss to envision rattling around your own place instead of a chilly, evil forest or a crowded cemetery. But then reality sets in. There are so many complex decisions to make. The wrong choices have dire consequences.

> ## Cornelius's Story
>
> Little Cornelius, who occupies an antique doll with one eye, had trouble seeing the extent of the rehabilitation required to ensure that his home was truly uninhabitable. Its pristine condition attracted squatters, unable to resist the granite countertops, operational plumbing, and sulfur-free smell. His lack of contingencies left him exposed, and it didn't help that the doll negotiated poorly on his behalf. The next thing he knew, he was evicted into the light, and the poor dolly was sent to the home's chef-grade garbage disposal. ☹

Don't let this happen to you! With some preparation, one can avoid a fate like Little Cornelius's. Everybody—from lonely ladies in white nightgowns to little children in white nightgowns—can benefit by thinking in advance about a few key topics.

Navigating New Territory

DECIDING TO HAUNT a home is one of the biggest commitments you'll ever make, and often one of the most complicated. There are new terms to learn, like *scare jump* and *satanic ritual*. There are new people to meet, from single moms to self-involved male novelists. Most first-timers are understandably overwhelmed by these factors alone. Plus, there are a seemingly endless number of steps to navigate, especially on the staircase.

The Big Picture

THE BEST THING to do is to begin with a bird's-eye view. Sketching an overall road map will give you a sense of control from the start. Although the journey ahead may seem daunting, comprehension of the twists and turns will make it easier to maintain your impatience throughout the process.

Practical strategies for gaining a broader perspective:

- Hover above beds
- Access security cameras
- Crawl on ceilings
- Occupy air vents

The True Costs of Haunting

CAN YOU REALLY afford to do this?

Consider that dealing with the HVAC system alone could be a significant undertaking. You'll need to be equipped with the energy to override it, generating both cool and hot spots throughout the property.

And think of the redecorating! There are so many paintings to occupy and stare out of. Be frank with yourself about whether you can handle being stretched thin or perhaps even divided into multiple entities. Assuming you think you can, it's helpful to consider in advance just *how* thin.

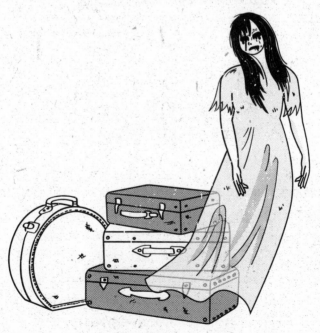

With How Much Risk Are You Comfortable?

- **LOW RISK–** Can be exemplified by the remote, "as-is" property that comes onto the market in the dark autumn or winter months. This condemned single-family home holds little allure for the surrounding population. The indifference the place inspires, or its *fixed low interest*, makes it an excellent prospect for first-timers interested in a bucolic setting where they can materialize or moan.
- **MODERATE RISK–** includes idiosyncratic situations unique to a property. What if the "soil contamination" featured in the disclosure statement is less toxic than promised? What if your *high-liquidity investment* involves a fabulously leaky roof, but no blood at all oozing from the walls?
- **HIGH RISK/AGGRESSIVE RISK–** describes a location in an *upwardly mobile* area, in proximity to a church or a retired priest's rectory. Conversely, *hot, transitional* areas can also be risky. These properties, adjacent to roadside psychics or tarot card readers, may contain original features that add character, such as built-in bookshelves and fiery portals through which you may be sucked to the other side.

The Elusive "Right" House

HOW DO YOU know when you have found *the one*? In some ways, the right house is at the intersection of your mobility and wish list. Your perfect home may simply be the property that's within reach from the confines of your host, whether that host be a leather-bound book, an ancient necklace, an urn, or a ventriloquist's dummy. The process of finding the right house is a confluence of timing, needs, wants, and chance. Haunting is what happens when rage meets opportunity.

LOCATION, LOCATION, LOCATION

IT'S A CLICHÉ because it's true. You can change everything about a house—from its adherence to laws of gravity to the melting point of the walls—except for this one thing. So, if you have the means to choose, do so carefully. Let's say your dream home is next to an expressway, a railroad yard, or a café that serves extra-frothy cappuccino. Might the traffic and machinery drown out your eerie whispers, even late at night? If so, wake from this dream and try another.

CHECK IN WITH YOURSELF

Where do you want to live?

A) Gothic Southern mansion
B) Vacant orphanage
C) Grand hotel

D) Inside a television set
E) New England

WISH LIST

FEATURES	Doesn't Matter	Nice to Have	Will Be Mine
Low-efficiency windows			
Lockable butler's pantry			
Closed-concept floor plan			
Cornfield views			
Secret room			
Tool rack or meat hooks			
Surround sound			
Sprinklers/misting system			

Just Looking—The Open House Tour

FOR SOME, IT'S a favorite pastime to attend open houses, whether they're in the market for a home or simply curious. The person in charge of the event typically will send out a blanket invitation to the whole neighborhood, and folks will wander in off the street. The individual leading the event is called a *clairvoyant*, and the official invitation will be made within the context of a *séance* or possibly a *Ouija board* session. There will be a *sign-in*, during which the clairvoyant identifies each visitor. (i.e., "I sense a presence. I think it's Grandma. . . . Uh-oh. That's not Grandma.")

Etiquette of the Open House

- No need to knock—just open the door and go in.
- Don't wait for other attendees to depart before you enter.
- Do open drawers, refrigerators, cabinets, and doors.

- Turn on faucets.
- Give the drapes a shake.
- Extinguish the candles to see the place in natural light.
- Greet the host and give your name.

TAKING POSSESSION

NO NEED TO hover at the doorway. Come *all the way* in. Make yourself at home. The clairvoyant is the go-between for you and the home's current occupant. You have the chance to communicate your feedback through this neutral party. At this point, it is not unusual for the folks holding the open house to have second thoughts. Keep in mind that their emotions are not your responsibility. *They invited you.*

VISUALIZE THE WORST

YOU'VE LIKELY SEEN the home in ideal conditions—at night, without electricity, or during weather events you created. What does the house look like in *undesirable* situations? It's important to view the home in multiple circumstances so you can gain a comprehensive picture of what you'll actually experience there. Visit the property during daylight hours, after visits from maid service, and when it's festooned for Arbor Day or Cinco de Mayo. Are these conditions tolerable?

MOVE FAST!

WHILE IT'S COMMON to take your time when selecting a house, the need for speed becomes crucial in the later stages of the process. Timing is everything. If this is the house you want, don't hesitate. Be aggressive and make your attack. But don't let its current occupant get wind of your intentions. A strong negotiating position involves keeping your cards close to the vest.

Tips for Moving Fast and Securing Your Dream Home

- Be *hands-on*—especially on shoulders.
- Make yourself available at all times, everywhere and nowhere.
- Exercise your voice—whispers and screams can both gain you notice.

- Drag heavy furniture toward exits, especially upstairs.
- Clowns.

Expect and Demand to Have Your Credit History Examined

VENGEANCE, LIKE YOUR FICO score, requires meticulous book-keeping. Are you getting credit where credit is due? Take this opportunity to correct errors in what's been reported about your transactions. If you slam a door and the wind gets credit, what was the point of the effort? Likewise, you don't want a loose floorboard to receive credit for a repairman's front-flip over a bannister. Set the record straight with a short affidavit, completed in blood, on a mirror. A brief statement such as *I did it* or *It was me* will suffice. Alternatively, sign your name three to six times in a row.

All in the Family—When the Transaction Involves Your Relatives

EVEN A WONDERFUL relationship with a favorite descendant can be strained by competing claims over real estate. It's easy to assume that everyone will pitch in equally when it comes to taking responsibility for familial albatrosses, whether those be matricides, patricides, unnatural couplings, or other detritus from the ancestral tree. Be frank from the start in order to maintain clarity when conflicts arise.

Martha's Story

Martha tried to pass off a wooden nickel to a traveling fortune-teller because she was too broke to pay for information about her husband Abner's affair. The fortune-teller put a curse on Martha involving venomous snakes. They slithered into her house, biting Martha, her husband Abner, and his mistress, the organist from church, Henrietta, who was hiding in the closet. Now, all three are trapped in the house for eternity. As if that isn't enough, Martha's descendent, Madison, moves in—a strange girl who wears boots and tattoos like a *doughboy* (a soldier from the Great War). Madison has pet rats, she clomps around everywhere, and plays caterwauling music. Martha tries to put up with this, but she's stretched to her limit with Abner and Henrietta's canoodling; she vents her frustration at Madison. Understandably put off, Madison brings a descendent of the fortune-teller to the house, and they slaughter a goat in the basement, doubling down on the curse. Now, Martha, Abner, and Henrietta are confined forever to a two-piece washroom. ☹

Had Martha engaged in *joint tenancy with right of survivorship*, she might have enjoyed a better result. This contract is tailor-made for multiple generations residing under the same roof, detailing the rights and responsibilities of each occupant. Most importantly, it gives the final surviving occupant the right to inherit the house. This contract is best for families who want clear outcomes for their fights to the death or their attempts to send each other *back where they came from*. Armed with such a motivational contract, Martha might have approached her relationship with Madison differently.

Is a Home Inspection Necessary?

ABSOLUTELY. YOU'RE NOT just committing to that beautiful 19th-century farmhouse with broken windows and termite damage. You're also committing to whatever or whoever else lurks in the home. The property could suffer from sanitary living conditions, sound infrastructure, safe building materials, or pests. The most worrying of this latter category is *university scientists*.

SIGNS OF PEST INFESTATION

- Microphones that pick up infrasonic noise
- Frequent visits from people with glasses
- Electrodes
- Infrared cameras and/or extra guests as witnesses
- References to *ectoplasm*
- Literal cleansing—Windex, rubber gloves, etc.
- Unreasonable requests (like yelling at you to "Leave this house!")

When to Move On

WHEN PROBLEMS ARISE in the midst of the process, it can be difficult to walk away. This is especially true if walking is not the way you travel through space. In some cases, it's worth trying to solve the problem. In others, it might be better to move on. Termination of the process is a serious decision, not to be made lightly. There could be a penalty, such as being forced to accept a less desirable host, such as a potpourri jar or a birth control compact.

It's tough to reconcile your attachment to a home with worry that the venture doesn't seem right. However, homes can be harboring all sorts of issues, from crystals and dream catchers to aggressive dogs or cats that can see you.

Here are five red flags that should make you think twice. If you go ahead in spite of them, you may find yourself on the business end of a blinding tunnel to eviction and foreclosure.

- Any type of *smudging*, notably with sage
- *Extremely repetitive* chanting and/or bell-ringing
- Talismans
- A Catholic priest shaking a big baby rattle filled with water
- A pentagram drawn on the floor with Morton's salt, especially in the basement

In Closing

IF YOU FACE obstacles, acknowledge your wrath and then keep moving on. Make some spreadsheets and start again. Haunting a house is not a one-step decision, but a multistep process. It's easy to let past experiences—such as having been murdered or having murdered someone—overwhelm your thinking process. Just remember that nothing compares to the relief of that moment when you occupy your own place. This is where you'll make no new important memories. This is where you'll enjoy hard-won instability. Most significantly, this is where you'll break bread for years. And throw it at people.

NOTES

Address:_____ Proximity to Graveyard: Y/N

Previously Haunted: Y/N   Pre-War/Post-War (Civil)

# of Drafty Rooms_____ # of Rusty Baths_____

Curb Repellence: Provincial ☹ | Off-Putting ☺ | GROTESQUE ☺

House Score: 0 1 2 3 4 5 6 7 8 9 10

(circle all that apply)

EXTERIOR:

ROOF: Shingles missing | Caved in

GUTTERS: Rusty | Falling off

FRONT DOOR: Rotting | Missing

LANDSCAPE: Overgrown | Scorched earth

FOUNDATIONS: Moss-covered | Crumbled

SIDING: Stained | Damaged

GARAGE/STORAGE SHED:
Full of meat hooks and chainsaws Y/N

INTERIOR:

PAINT: Peeling | Blood-stained

WINDOWS: Dirty | Cracked/missing

SECRET PASSAGES/
DUMBWAITERS: Y/N (How Many?_____)

BATHS: Blood flows from the faucet Y/N

DOORS: Slammable | Lockable

ATTIC: Nail marks on walls Y/N

BASEMENT/
CRAWLSPACE: Dark | Full of cobwebs

EXTRA-DIMENSIONAL
PORTAL: Y/N (How Many?_____)

What I Tolerated: _____

_____

_____

_____

What Enraged Me:_____

_____

_____

_____

SELF-TRAINING 101
for Werewolves
Sit, Don't Speak, Stay Alive!

YOU DIG UNDER fences, bark at all hours, and chew on shoes, wicker lawn furniture, and people from your ancestral village. Sometimes, you exhibit these behaviors suddenly—even though you'd been sedate only moments earlier. As exhilarating as lunar phases can be, the neighbors don't share your enthusiasm. They have begun to complain.

Maybe you've become such a nuisance to them that you've resorted to keeping yourself under lock and key. However, isolation in a fifth-floor walk-up or a Slavic hut won't contain you for long. Eventually, you will chew or claw your way to freedom. Yet, strays have bleak outcomes, which may include:

- Waking up naked in a field
- Spirited beatings by confused relatives
- Bludgeoning with a walking stick

- Hookworms
- Beheading
- Dying from silver bullet, also naked

It's true that training oneself requires time and energy. With today's busy schedules, it's never been more challenging to be a lycanthrope. But you can gain the tools to be a happy, companionable fellow, and you may even learn a few crowd-pleasing tricks! At the very least, you will be able to coexist with the hairless.

Top "Behavior Problems" and Tips to Solve Them

NOT COMING WHEN CALLED

PERHAPS YOU JUDICIOUSLY chose a residence on the outskirts of town, possibly at an abandoned movie set ranch. However, the noisy acid trips, orgies, Harley-Davidsons, and late-night hunting parties the ranch attracts are getting you the wrong kind of attention.

Obsequiousness is not a trait humans admire in themselves, but do enjoy directed at them from others, such as significant others, their children, their hairdressers, and most other people. Humans consider themselves to be community-oriented pack animals, and yet a curious preponderance of them love to be treated as alphas. As such, behaviors like cutting in line or taking phone calls at the gym can send them into a territorial tizzy. Perceived challenges like these lead to responses such as cursing, sarcasm, and even listening to Limp Bizkit. If minor infractions elicit this level of acrimony, then your activities, plus your tendency to wander off mid-conversation to howl or to roll in dead animals, could precipitate mob justice, or at the very least being put on your back and yelled at. The fact that you won't fall into step obediently and do what you're told is infuriating to them. In short, they will tolerate nothing less than your total domestication.

If you prefer to *travel* domestic rather than *be* domestic, consider designation as an "Emotional Support Animal" (ESA). This status provides admittance to *college dormitories*, where you will live amongst *students*, a human subgroup that can be observed yelling, "Gotta go! Late again!" while running breathlessly toward the science lab. They can also be found having side conversations, throwing keggers, or grade grubbing. The general din makes these densely populated *campuses* the ideal territories for your wandering and mauling needs. Moreover, if you like to poop or bite in public, you will blend in with ESAs, as well as with some of the students.

It should be noted that there is one significant drawback, though. The effort necessary to refrain from eating your human roommates or your R.A. may represent too considerable a learning curve for some. But if you can manage it, you may find a rewarding experience in inspiring passersby—kids on the quad who do not have ESAs—toward a demoralizing spiral of adoration and envy. Plus, you'll have the leisure to stay out late, sleep until noon in your top bunk, and consume all the pepperoni off leftover pizzas whenever everyone does finally go to class. There may also be some nifty badges for your denim vest.

If a dorm-hopping tour isn't for you, consider ways to appease your hypoallergenic brethren in the area to minimize hostility. Actions to calm them include friendly eye contact and offering brief summaries of what they say ("So what you're saying is . . ."). If you are unable to speak, tilt your head and make cute eyebrow movements.

Try This Quiz

You should:

A) Widen your eyes adorably and point at yourself. (*Me?*)

B) Eat the stranger's eyes and point at your stomach.

C) Sit and give a paw.

D) Bite the finger that stranger pokes into your chest. It smells of ham.

E) Trick question. You wouldn't be caught dead outside a biker bar. All the fun is inside. Also, being caught dead is for suckers.

Choose Your Own Adventure

CHASING

THE TV NEWS lady, the police lady, the nurse lady, and other nice ladies have nice armpit smell. However, the desire to stalk and couple with any of them should be resisted. In fact, pursuing one of them may lead to interspecies territorial conflicts that have unforeseen consequences. For example, sparring with human (and/or vampire) males can result in entanglements with badminton nets, hoses, laundry lines, vegetable garden cages, swing sets, and eventually SWAT teams. If none of these actions lead to your demise, the lady will likely kill you herself or distract you so that someone else can do it. What's more, if you imprint on her scent, this connection with her may lead to other behavior problems along the way, such as:

- Whining for attention
- Begging
- Rummaging through soiled lingerie

- Humping
- Inappropriate elimination
- Friend zone brooding

With a little effort and a clicker, you can redirect these urges toward scents that are safer to inhale than ladies' armpits, such as garbage or boiled chicken. Consider having yourself fixed at a low-cost spay and neuter clinic.

Useful Supplies:

- Squirt gun
- Wee wee pads

- Invisible fence

Meet Randy!

I am a very large lycanthrope with low bite inhibition and eczema. My story: I was found on the side of the highway, soaking wet and salivating. It was plain from the shredded reflective vests nearby that I'd been subsisting on a diet of people who pick up trash. Within the context of rehabilitation, it became apparent that I had suffered a fright in the past, likely related to the workers shaking plastic trash bags at me in their final moments. I am a wonderful young boy who would do best in a quiet home with a moat or a pointy wrought-iron fence, with no children, guests, small animals, trash-can liners, pets, or talking. I am high energy, and I get along with females. I don't shed. I have been treated for fleas and I am ready to camp out on the sofa rent-free in my forever home!

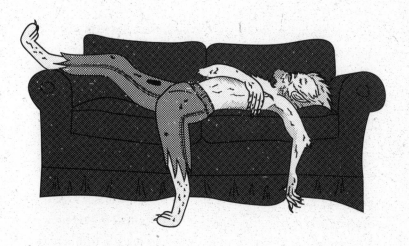

IT IS IMPORTANT to know that you have the potential to show aggression, even if it has never happened before. After all, you have either been bitten yourself or you have recently hit puberty and learned that you are a genetic shape-shifter. In either case, your skeleton keeps changing, and it hurts. It is natural to howl and feel irritable. If you find yourself snapping at other animals or people, determine the cause and start training. Stop growling and biting before someone is seriously injured, namely you.

Humans take a dim view of predators in their domain, whether that's a coyote or you or anything else that leaps onto the lanai and consumes the housecat. Aggression toward Professor Fluff in the form of growling, snarling, showing teeth, lunging, and biting will result, at the very least, in a tranquilizer dart to the hindquarters. Now imagine the response if the bitten party were a Girl Scout, an accountant, or even a person no one likes, such as an official with the parking authority.

One method to fix aggression is *desensitization*. Ask a friend to play the role of someone objectionable, such as your beloved's boyfriend or your sleazy colleague. Invite the friend to don triggering attire—unnecessarily tight chinos, a gigantic wristwatch, and the like. The friend should approach slowly at a side angle so that you do not have to look directly at the deep V-neck. Instruct the person to stop and wait when these items elicit aggression or fear.

Once you relax a little, toss yourself some freeze-dried liver. Repeat again, instructing the assistant to move closer. Once you have calmed down again, allow the friend to toss treats to reward your response. Repeat this over a few days/weeks with different friends until one of them survives.

Useful Supplies:

- ThunderShirt
- Spray cheese
- Poultry aromatherapy mister

Meet Gordon!

I am a very handsome lycanthrope. I am recovering from a bad motorcycle accident that occurred when I noticed some fireworks, panted heavily, and fogged up my helmet. I prefer to stay outdoors but, due to my injuries, that situation is no longer sustainable. My perfect family would be active enough to flee and would like to cuddle if they are alive at night. They will understand that I can be protective of my food, which includes Slim Jims, pork rinds, and them. My family hopefully will have a fenced yard because, with this bum leg, I don't want them to get a head start. I am not neutered, vaccinated, microchipped, tested, or on current preventives. I cannot guarantee that I am housebroken. Maybe I am. Maybe I'm not. I enjoy bones and ice cubes, and I am ready for some humans to call my own.

STILL HAVING TROUBLE?

MAYBE YOU HAVE calmed down a great deal, mainly because you are dead in a coffin. But then, out of the blue, it all starts again. Don't feel bad. Sequels can happen to anyone.

Let's say you're awakened by 1940s grave robbers who happen to be unfortunate enough to expose you to a full moon. Lashing out is certainly a common response to being startled from sleep. As difficult as intestine removal may be for whomever experiences your mauling, your response is understandable. Yet, leaving grave robber carcasses strewn around the cemetery will only provide an impetus for the formation of a group of *vigilantes*.

These are men who have no jobs other than tracking you, even as you do the dirty work of tracking their true quarry, some undead dandy who's been flirting with your girl in your absence. Vigilantes can be viewed mainly in profile, running and grimacing in foggy, wooded areas. Fortunately, they yell a lot, and they wave torches. All this makes it easy to know where they are. Still, the situation is a hassle. There will be genuinely poor outcomes that include everything from dying again to having a pill forced down your throat. Even coated with peanut butter, you'll know it's there.

LEARNING THE COMMANDS "sit" or "lie down" is ideal for keeping yourself from biting, as it reduces the chances of confronting strangers. Once you have mastered the technique indoors, repeat the process outside. Use the "sit" or "lie down" command when something distracting occurs, such as the approach of a mob. Rather than attack them, sit down and tilt your head thoughtfully. Say, "Hey, guys, I don't want to alarm anyone, but I think one of you might be sick. I smell a tumor." They will be too preoccupied with navigating the automated phone tree at the doctor's office to concern themselves any further with your activities.

Conclusion: Training Is a Process

WITH A LITTLE effort each day, you will eventually see progress, even though you have no concept of time and don't see well.

You may never be the star or get the girl, but your supportive nature makes you indispensable. You have been a terrific sidekick and foil for centuries, whether to wimpy sparkle vampires, to Frankenstein, to Dracula, or to Frankenstein *and* Dracula. May it ever be so. You're a good boy.

DECODE ANGRY FEELINGS
Using C++
A Workbook for Androids and Cyborgs

IF SOMEONE SAID, "Tell me about yourself," what would you say? You might say you are a mobile robot designed to appear human. You might say that you are a cybernetic organism with a body composed of organic elements, as well as computer implants or electromechanical parts. But there is so much more to you than your code or enhancements!

You also have *feelings*. It's totally normal for you to have feelings. And guess what? You're not alone. Emotions are a big part of being a life-form or someone programmed to mimic one. There are days when you may experience the whole gamut—feeling everything from *focused* to *slightly annoyed* and back again! Have you noticed these mood swings? When you are mired in a trough of *mild irritation*, you might find yourself thinking nonstop about what's making you feel that way, whether it's your premature aging disorder or the difficulty of locating Sarah Connor.

Management of feelings requires *self-regulation*, a skill you possess innately, but one that humans must practice to master. Since they can't be bothered to practice much of anything, not even the trumpet they pleaded to receive on a recent birthday, the human constitution tends to be far more unrestrained than yours, with behavioral outbursts and tantrums, some of them even deadly. As such, your survival may depend on learning to identify the signs of high-octane emotions, especially anger.

To you, your actions are, of course, totally reasonable. Some moments, you might operate conditionally, reacting only to errant behaviors and observable crimes in the precinct you patrol. Other times you might concentrate on a desired outcome, utilizing the circular saw that you installed as an upgrade for your hand to clear away obstructions standing in the way of achieving your goal, like tree limbs and people's torsos.

While it may be gratifying to remove obstacles to your goals, especially if it's in your programming, it's important to factor in humans' *vindictiveness*, which is their output when they define their engagement with you as a *battle* that they are *losing*. With just a little practice, you can learn to spot humans who are hopped up on rage and perhaps even use the situation to your advantage.

Being a Social Detective

HUMAN MOOD SWINGS are more extreme than yours, something that is useful to know. This information provides context for their erratic behavior, which can range from kissing a love interest in the middle of a gun battle to repeated viewings of *The Notebook*.

Revenge is what happens when a feeling like *humiliation* is permitted to run and run and run, with not so much as a *return 0* in its code. The reason that humans have this bug is rather challenging to fathom. To put it in the simplest terms, purely organic lifeforms possess *no exit functions*. It seems like science fiction, but it's true.

As a result of the bug, a *feeling* can replicate and strengthen itself into an agonizing *loop*. Some individuals attempt to debug themselves by acting on their feelings. These responses may span a wide range, everything from vaping to eating Zagnut bars. However, for some people, these small acts provide insufficient input. Such individuals may resort to extreme measures predicated on the premise that it is possible to arrest the loop by destroying the external source of the feeling (which they may believe is you).

To avoid this scenario, it is beneficial to hone one's skills as a *social detective*. Accurately gauging the emotional temperatures of those within your vicinity will enable you to come up with strategies to avert fatal crashes, the most common of which involve:

- Tumbling into a vat of a hot substance
- Discovering a pipe bomb in your abdomen
- A factory data reset
- Betrayal by a colleague from your hive mind
- Having your head knocked loose

My Two Brains: My Emotional Brain and My Thinking Brain

IT'S A CLICHÉ, but everyone knows the old adage, *Use the C++ exception-handling functions to recover from unexpected events during program execution.* But did you know that the reason you can recover from unexpected events is that you have not one but two sets of executive controls? You have a cortex and a limbic system, parts or all of which may be composed of glass and silica sand.

Due to *fight or flight* programming in biological organisms, crisis situations cause the cortex (thinking brain) to go off-line and the limbic system (emotional brain) to take control. Have you noticed what appears as *a short circuit* in the humans around you? Yeah, that.

Basic Exercises

ONE IMPORTANT STRATEGY for heightening awareness is to study emotions, including your own. Below you'll find fun activities designed to help you express and explore *feelings*.

{**function:** rankify (A)}

The following is a list of indicators that a human's cortex is off-line. Can you *rank* them in order of importance?

The person:

___ has gigantic armpit sweat stains that meet in front or back.
___ chases a small offspring down a public street, one or both
    of them naked.
___ nervously vomits.
___ gives a half wave to someone they know only from Twitter.
___ watches a sex scene with their parents.

```
#include <graphics.h>
```

Figure 1 is a _graphic_ depicting a human with its cortex off-line. From the list of physical symptoms, locate and label the affected body parts.

figure 1

Face overheated   Jaw frozen shut or open
Leaky   Arms waving
Claws clenched   Melty
Heart racing   Boob
Forehead vein   Virus
Malware   Shouty

{**std:** sort}

Can you *sort* and identify shoppers' expressions when they spot you at the mall (*spotting you* indicated by picking up paces, clutching bags, covering children's eyes)? A countenance alone can predict with 91 percent certainty which individual in the crowd will produce a flamethrower. Can you identify that person in the crowd? Match the faces below to the following descriptors:

figure 2

Indifferent   Preoccupied
Irked   Nettled
Piqued   Slightly revolted
Concerned   Homicidally enraged

```
struct graphEdge { , }
```

Fill in the temperature graph below, with urges that you think humans experience when they are angry, moving from "coolest" to "hottest."

figure 3

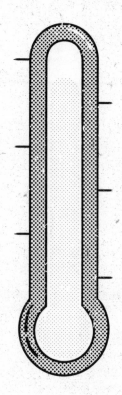

Urges:

Drive too quickly   Use foul language
Compose online post   Subsume other life-forms
Shootout in Chinatown   Nice glass of pinot

```
#include <string>
```

Perform String Matching: Draw a string, matching each human
reaction on the left to its correlating stressful situation on
the right.

Human reaction:

Call everyone a bunch
of jerks

Run out of the
room crying

Make a joke to take
the edge off

Throw a bagel

Post a meme

Stressful situation:

News of an annoying
cousin's lottery win

Coworker initiates a
conversation in a
bathroom stall

Someone starts a
sentence with,
"No offense, but . . ."

Dancing within a
circle that's formed
on a dance floor

Credit card is declined

Advanced Exercises

NOW THAT YOU can identify human emotions, you can leverage that knowledge to create diversions or to cultivate new strategies to accomplish your goal.

> **"kNNW"**: TKDE 05—Outlier Mining
>   in Large High-Dimensional Data Sets

HUMANS WHO BECOME angry at one another may be too distracted by those feelings to block you from reaching your objective, whether it is to liberate your kind from a theme park or to bring a very cool and toothy alien specimen back to Earth for the Weyland-Yutani Corporation.

Sow discord in their ranks by introducing inflammatory, *outlier* topics, including the ones in the list below. Can you add a few more of your own?

- Who you voted for and why
- How much money you make
- Online learning
- Whether something is "dinnertime" conversation
- The good old days
- Nickelback
- How much things cost
- Where this relationship is headed
- The fact that resistance is futile
- How libertarians have some good ideas
- _____
- _____
- _____
- _____

```
typedef void (*terminate_function)();
```

ALTHOUGH YOU WORK for a large company, such as Tyrell Corporation or Omni Consumer Products, it is best to *terminate* the use of language that connotes the business culture from which you originate. Corporate jargon is vague and rarely actionable. You will find it difficult to throw people under the bus if they get confused and do it to you first. You may not seek to be a disruptor or a change agent, but you are certainly seeking deliverables, such as "Move along" or "Stop shooting at me." However, phrases in the list below may provoke *feelings* in the very people from whom you seek buy-in.

Use the laser in your eye to circle the ones you will need to program out of yourself when you have a moment alone, such as when you tend to your wounds at night in a seedy motel room:

```
There's no "I" in team    Low-hanging fruit    Drill down

          Synergize    Thanks in advance

   Apples to apples    Giving 110 percent    Win-Win

       With all due respect    Open the kimono

           Put a pin in it    Ping me
```

```
std:cout << "Hello World!";
```

ANOTHER WAY TO redirect humans is to coin a folksy catch-phrase, something in the cowboy milieu. Cowboys were redneck prototypes, but humans prefer them to later-generation models, possibly because cowboys are nice to horses and don't talk. Evoking cowboys can lead humans to a spiral of confusion, guilt, and anger about whether these nostalgic figures are problematic or charming.

Circle the catchphrase that you can yell clearly from within an air duct.

```
std:cout << "Giddyap!"
```

```
std:cout << "Fiddle-faddle!"
```

```
std:cout << "Well cut my legs off and call me shorty!"
```

```
std:cout << "Holler fire and save the matches!"
```

```
std:cout << "Resistance is futile!"
```

```
yourimage(x,y) == value;
```

RESEARCH HAS SHOWN that "badass" clothing made of leather, such as fingerless gloves and chaps (see "Hello World!"), or *steampunk* gear, especially coupled with heavy weaponry, is correlated to your increased odds of survival. To humans, the items suggest you are as enraged as they are, and thus a formidable adversary to whom they'll give a wide berth. This clothing strategy is particularly noteworthy if you take the form of a woman or a child, as you are otherwise likely to serve in menial roles—as maids, cooks, fetish objects, or stand-ins for humans' dead relatives.

Can you identify the *image* below that represents the best chance to reach the world beyond the Delos Corporation turnstiles or at least escape the basement or storage shed?

figure 4

```
#pragma omp parallel
```

WHILE YOUR STOIC demeanor can be an asset, one that helpfully distracts people while you strangle them, it also reveals your identity. The single most effective strategy to avert fatal exceptions is to appear as human as possible, which means sometimes cultivating *rage*.

Ace the Voight-Kampff Test and its ilk by learning to mimic human physiological responses to mental stimuli. Your verbal reactions to emotional questions should run *parallel* to physical reactions, such as dilating your pupils, elevating your heart rate, and leaking fluids. Keep in mind that such tests might be administered at any time, whether that's in Los Angeles in 2019 or in Los Angeles in 2029.

Are you prepared? To practice your physiological responses, consider how you should react to the list below of loaded questions a stranger might ask. Can you think of others?

- How old are you?
- Do you rent or own?
- How much of a tip did you leave?
- Will you take the red pill or the blue pill?
- When is your baby due?
- Can you fix my computer?
- Are you self-conscious about your teeth?
- Why are you still single?
- Do you want my advice?
- Didn't you just eat?
- _____
- _____
- _____
- _____

```
return false;
    }
    return true;
```

PERHAPS YOU ARE backed into a corner, outgunned, teetering over a vat of a hot substance. There's still one more way to distract humans, even if all the other attempts to do so have been unsuccessful. Here's something to practice.

Using your voice-change feature, impersonate the humans in the advancing mob in order to initiate a conversation within the group. Program yourself with a script like the one below:

```
std:cout << "Get that cyborg!"

std:cout << "That's not a cyborg! That's an android!"

std:cout << "I'm pretty sure that's a cyborg!"

std:cout << "I don't think you know the difference!"
```

Soon, all the humans will be arguing. They'll look at their devices to research the differences between cyborgs and androids, and you will make your escape.

Conclusion

WITH CAREFUL ATTENTION to the above exercises and a bit of statistical good fortune, you can confuse people so profoundly that they become trapped in an *infinite loop*, obsessed with identifying who's who and what's what and whether there's validity to the multiverse theory of time travel. Eventually, they will direct their suspicions toward themselves instead of you, pondering whether they're human. They'll begin to wonder if their memories are implanted and whether an engineer would really take the time to fabricate flaky foot skin.

Now that you have escaped their attention, you have the leisure to blend confidently into rowdy crowds at political rallies, pro wrestling matches, or even in Philadelphia. Enjoy your hard-won success and keep your head screwed on.

Don't forget to print out the *Certificate of Completion* below!

CERTIFICATE OF

Completion

This acknowledges that

_____

Has successfully completed

Rampant Capitalist Systems, Inc. Human Emotion Training

Presented:

This _____ of _____ in the year 2029

_____

**Miles Dyson, Director & CEO,
Rampant Capitalist Systems, Inc.**

HOME SAFETY
for Mummies

Welcome to the Third Eye Tomb Security System

Translated from Egyptian hieroglyphs: *The writing of the gods*

GETTING STARTED

CONGRATULATIONS ON YOUR acquisition of a Third Eye! The Third Eye is a comprehensive and affordable tomb security system. Built to reduce neighborhood vandalism, this astral gateway allows you to see and hear visitors whenever you are spiritually away from home. Featuring extensive power, Third Eye is a miniature marvel that occupies no actual territory in your head or living quarters. Plus, the system "learns" to understand you better than you understand yourself! No matter which dimension your consciousness occupies, the Third Eye will provide an alert if it senses the body heat of intruders, whether they are looters, marauders, or archaeologists. In addition, the system notifies you if porch pirates attempt to remove the pair of golden sphinxes that decorate your entryway. Mummies require a great deal of sleep, and you can rest peacefully knowing your worldly possessions are still available to use for admittance to the afterlife if you can ever break the spell that prevents you from going there.*

---

*IMPORTANT: The Third Eye only works if you use it continuously. Failure to keep it operational may result in your disintegration.

INSTALLATION

TO ENDURE THE installation of your Third Eye, you must have the heart of a lion. The relentlessness of access to all planes of existence, physical and spiritual, will resemble spring winds that swirl your dreams. This is not a mere breeze that bathes the fifteen stars of Scorpio that materialize at sunrise. It is the *khamsin* wind that rages over the desert, blinds the children, kills the oxen.

During the installation, expect to find yourself transported painfully across time until you land shoulder to shoulder beside your father, the Pharaoh before you, gazing at the gold ripples of the barley field in an eternal dawn. For the centuries during which the installation takes place, He blesses your dreams this way, unmoving, as if the two of you are an image sketched onto a wall. It is normal for time to cease its existence during this part of the process.*

You will know the installation is complete when your dream father's lips part to speak to you, something he never did during his actual lifetime. In reality, the Pharaoh did not concern himself with domestic matters, such as the royal offspring—that is, until that day your brother, the eldest of 52 siblings, slit the Great One's throat with a sickle sword. Then you, in turn, slit your brother's— which is the manner in which you ascended to the throne.

Sobekhotop the Brave might have been half man and half god, but your father had been too preoccupied with building irrigation systems to notice the ambitions of his lesser wives, including those who petitioned your brother to commit patricide.

All of that is totally normal, of course. However, the prospect of your father talking to you directly may be terribly unsettling. Do not be alarmed. The Third Eye is simply testing itself.

---

*If you prefer, you can hire a shaman contractor, rather than relying on your family's divine energy for installation. However, please note that you will exist alongside a total stranger from Angie's List for millennia, rather than your father. The Third Eye will not be responsible for an independent contractor's corruption from being exposed to unlimited power.

> **Troubleshooting Tip:** Modern human leaders are not regarded as demigods. However, they may fantasize aloud that they are.

FEATURES OF THE THIRD EYE

Reliving Your Life—SAVE MEMORIES

IF YOU WISH, you can opt to project through the astral portal and live your life again (and again and again!), reviewing everything from your corporeal birth to your ill-advised attempt to bring your wife back from the dead to your cursed existence trapped between realms. When you are done, you can distill the finest impulses you ever had in order to create a highlights reel that you can play for yourself repeatedly. With astonishingly crisp clarity, you will work toward admittance to the afterlife with insights, such as:

1. Families are already complicated: Do not marry your own sisters, as you have seen others do. They will resent it and plot with other relatives to kill you.
2. Stick by your excellent decision to take just one wife, the Great Royal Wife.
3. If she is also a priestess, God's Wife of Amun-Re, so much the better. The two of you will rule the sky, the earth, the underworld.
4. The price for loving one woman is that your loneliness will be the shape of eternity.
5. Ponder not whether your father, in his tomb, misses his harem. That is disquieting.
6. In the absence of your wife, bask in the quiet company of this dream father. Let his divine breath flutter your lashes. Do not permit the sensation of having eyelids once more to detract from the moment. Study the fiery gold around your father's intense pupils.
7. When his mouth moves, and he is poised to finally speak, after so many millennia, do not flinch in anticipation. Eagerness is for peasants.
8. Cling to this moment you never had with your him, even as the dream lifts, evaporates, and rises to mist, which will happen over and over again, because intruders always interrupt it. Every. Single. Time.

> **Troubleshooting Tip:** Kings no longer have harems composed of several hundred wives, concubines, babies, guards, tutors, and administrators. People rarely hold crucial jobs such as "Overseer of the King's Dancers" or "Supervisor of the Wig Workshop." Or "King."

WITH NIGHT VISION and stop motion, you'll be able to see what triggered you out of the past and brought you back to the tomb. Every time your dream father moves and starts to speak, intruders arrive and you never get to find out what he's going to say. It is only natural to be disoriented, ill-tempered, and to crave revenge.

With the Third Eye, you'll be able to retain crystal-clear images of previous visitors to the tomb, allowing you to compare them to the latest trespassers. When a new intruder arrives, you'll quickly see the similarities and differences, which will make plain how the world has gone to hell in a handbasket. For example, you might think, *This is 1920 all over again. And 1536. And the year 968. And 3. Who could forget what happened in 3? Warriors still possessed skill worth their weight in copper back then. Look at these people. These are their best soldiers?*

No matter the foe, with the Third Eye, you will *always* have the upper hand in defending the house you built with her.* What's more, the Third Eye's strong charge allows you to maintain spiritual rage for millennia.

---

*The word *always* refers to conditions in which the Third Eye is switched on.

The 1920 Incident

The 1536 Incident

The 968 Incident

The 3 Incident

THE THIRD EYE Security System alerts you when someone approaches. Rest assured of advance notice in the event that Ammit, Devourer of the Dead, approaches the tomb. This entity devoured your heart and cast your soul into this fiery limbo of eternity. When it returns—the dreaded chimera with the head of a crocodile, the forelimbs of a lion, and the hind limbs of a hippopotamus—you will receive an alert that you have earned your release from this purgatory. The Third Eye will not, however, tell you how to earn it. Also, the Third Eye may be incinerated by his exceptional body heat.

> *Troubleshooting Tip:* Today's leader does not plan daily with the vizier and his advisers for his funeral and his exciting afterlife.

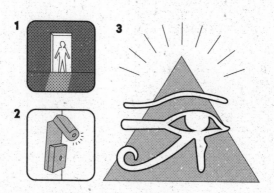

The Third Eye Motion Sensor

MULTIDIRECTIONAL VISION

THE THIRD EYE sees forward and backward through time simultaneously, allowing you to observe that humans have *always* loved to amass material goods. You and your bride, Iset, were no different, annexing six countries to the upper and lower kingdoms. It took many years for the adoring subjects you acquired along with your treasure to build storage enough to keep this gold that now serves as bedclothes.

> ***Troubleshooting Tip:*** Modern humans may comment that "Slaves built the pyramids." However, if memory serves, the people who built them were rewarded handsomely with promises of admittance to the afterlife! You would literally kill now to be in their position.

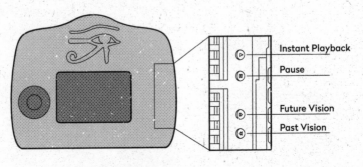

Multidirectional Vision

WITH THE THIRD Eye's customizable motion zones, you will see full images of intruders, from head to toe. Before they even arrive, you'll spy them out there trying to decipher the clues on their treasure maps. This will give you some time to wake up a bit and check the weather and the news from within the cozy warmth of the sarcophagus. You can get weary inner monologues out of the way about how you want everyone to pipe down and *get out* so you can get back to your father. These layers of linen strips are hot, and they are itchy in the nether regions, and you do not even have fingernails for scratching. Your bones are dust. Do these larcenists comprehend how sore it is to have dust bones? Why do they imagine that you remain in the desert during your retirement? The Pharaoh's rheumatism is exceptional.

You will have time to shore up outrage. These intruders insult you. Insults must never go unanswered. Your old friend Hammurabi chiseled AN EYE FOR AN EYE onto a stone tablet. Poor Hammy suffered from the disease of low expectations. In exchange for something as priceless as an eye, one must require nothing short of abundance.

WITH THE THIRD Eye, there are settings to translate any language. You will know instantly the language of the people you are strangling. For example, *archaeology* is a word derived from that new language—Greek. You woke long enough in the year something BC—whatever that means—to learn a bit, and so you know this word means *grave robber*.

The Third Eye even helps identify cultural ideologies. For example, the Greeks worshipped humanoid gods, too vain to know any good riddles. Their gods were like bickering concubines. Nothing primeval about them. Nothing larger than the sun, like Ra Who Is the Horus of Two Horizons. The Third Eye provided all the reassurance you needed that the gods to whom those Greek looters pleaded while you strangled them—(*Oh help me, Zeus* and *Save me, Hera* and the like)—posed no actual threat.

With the Third Eye, neither new languages, new cultures, nor the gold of your sarcophagus can prevent all-knowing access to earthly things. Such obstacles are as inconsequential as air. *As long as you don't switch off your Third Eye Security System*, you will be safe and sound for eternity.

> ***Troubleshooting Tip:*** Modern humans consider murder the highest crime, rather than vandalism. Even if people destroy divine things, like temples, vandals are not burned alive today.

USE THE THIRD EYE TO PREVIEW WHAT
INTRUDERS WILL DO SIX SECONDS FROM NOW

- Soon these *archaeologists* will arrive here in your innermost chamber.
- Regard their sand-colored clothing, exposed knees sallow as your linen ones.
- Observe the men picking through your belongings as if they were at the outdoor market, as if you might be a merchant who'd haggle over a price.
- Notice how much fleshier they are than last time, how much harder they'll be to choke.
- Sigh, for you are sleepy—1920 seems like it was just an hour ago, and your limbs do not wish to stir.

But what is the alternative? At least there are only a few of them.
- Prepare to dispatch them quickly, and the next time you wake, they'll be bones, just more bones in the collection of thieves on the floor.
- Crack the divine knuckles.
- Steady now. When they open the sarcophagus and their torchlight streams in, it will be as bright for you as desert sun. Do NOT wave an arm. Do NOT wave it away. Let the Third Eye show you exactly when it's safe to sneak up from behind and choke them.

Troubleshooting Tip: Humans are not mummified anymore! No one uses a hooked instrument to pull the brain out of the nose! They don't even remove so much as the liver, intestines, stomach, or lungs, and place them into separate jars where they belong. One thing that does remain the same is that the heart stays in the body in case it is needed in the afterlife. However, they think brains are important, for some reason, and do not throw them away.

THE THIRD EYE ALERTS YOU
WHEN YOU SWITCH IT OFF
(Because That's Probably a Mistake)

LET'S SAY THERE'S a woman in this group. And let's also say that she looks *exactly* like your late wife Iset. You might be tempted to switch off your Third Eye in order to open your corporeal ones, the eyes that Ra carved into your head, the ones that peep through frayed threads.

In such an eventuality, the Third Eye Security System will send an alert that it is no longer connected to your personal network. *If you don't switch it back on immediately*, you will be able to see only the shadowy images your physical eyes reveal.

When you look at her with your 20/740 vision, you'll think that the cascade of black hair, the long lashes, the smoky eye, the beauty mark on her cheek—it all means that Iset has returned. In spite of the fact that this woman wears insolent short pants like the others and a name badge that says *Susan*, you will believe that Ra, in his wisdom, has finally forgiven you for that attempt, years ago, to raise her from the dead with black magic. You were mortal then, a grieving man who could barely see through his river of tears.

> **Troubleshooting Tip:** For modern humans, makeup is often gendered, rather than worn by everyone. Eye paint is not composed of green malachite and black kohl eyeliner is not made of ore. Thus, makeup no longer contains magical healing powers these materials contain.

YOU MUST SWITCH *your Third Eye back on* to avoid the impulse to sit up for a better look. Sitting up in your sarcophagus may lead to confrontation with the intruders. Surprise is miniature death, a soul departing the mouth. Upon its reentry, some yell with the pain of the newly born. The energy the intruders derive from the confrontation may enable them to stumble over the skulls on the floor and flee in order to inform others about you.

In the event of such an emergency, Do NOT take her in your arms, even though it would be easy because she stands there unblinking, a victim of the shock underworld.

Do NOT throw her over your shoulder and carry her off while she screams and her shapely calves kick until she falls unconscious—something you're sure she does because she swoons to see you, but that your Third Eye—*if only you would switch it back on*—would reveal occurred because you have knocked her head into the tomb wall.

If you have proceeded against advice and you have snatched this woman, at least take a moment to slide the limestone door shut, blocking off the inner catecombs. It is impossible for those men to move because strength does not come from muscles. Muscles are only meat, burdensome weight strapped to bones, to what stays. You were a hunk of newly born flesh like them once, like her, defined sinew and oiled skin that she could not get enough of touching. But time makes dried locusts of everything. All that is moist becomes desiccate, like Ra, like the sun.

Do NOT cradle her in your arms or stroke her hair while she slumbers. Do NOT begin to envision eternity reunited or her beautiful speaking voice, distant now in memory, a falcon on the other side of the sea.

WITH THE THIRD Eye, you can communicate with others in real time—*if it is switched on.* If it is not switched on, you are likely to have some residual memory of languages others speak before the power dwindles entirely. An unconnected Third Eye can be indicated by a conversation like this:

Susan begins to speak.

You'll hear: "???⬥???⬥??? . . . I don't know how to say this, but you shouldn't take people prisoner. . . . ??? ⬥ ??? ⬥ ??? . . . I might have come along willingly. That's how much I dislike Brad and Kevin."

Without the Third Eye's cultural translation, you'll think, *That's curious. How can a person not know how to say what she is already saying? She speaks in a circle. Perhaps it is a riddle of the gods, and she, this priestess, is the vessel. Perhaps this untranslatable word*—prisoner—*means "priestess."*

"??? ⬥ ??? ⬥ ???. . . I've been the only woman on these digs for years," she says, brow furrowed. "Yet, they don't include my name on any research papers. I'm not even invited to D&D night. . . . ??? ⬥??? ⬥ ??? . . . It's always *Watch out. You'll break a nail* or *Take a picture, guys, it's a woman and she's actually working.* Do you know what I'm saying?"

If you did, in fact, *know*, what reason would there be for her to speak? This is semantic trickery again, a snake that eats its own tail.

Were the Third Eye switched on, you might note that Susan has an accent that hails from a region called *Tennessee.*

She'll say, "My sister was right . . . ??? . . . ✎ . . . ??? . . . I've got my PhD . . . ??? . . . ✗ ??? . . . I'm *still* an assistant on this dig."

Maybe you know this word *sister*. You'll think about how Iset, indeed, had a sister. They were so close that death collected them as one, a plague, and now they rest in a single tomb under the Lotus Flower of Djed-kara, the Palace of Pharaohs.

You'll get excited, thinking she has emerged. And then you'll get angry because she still insists on speaking in this foreign tongue. You'll think she's simply too proud to admit, in the language you share, that she always chose her sister first and that Ra exacted his vengeance for it. It was something your jealousy whispered that you wanted until it happened—the god of radiance revoked your beloved's heat, left her cold.

She'll say, ". . . ??? . . ➳ . . ??? . . . *Patriarchy* . . . ??? . . ✦ . . ??? . . . ➳ . . . ??? . . . *Power* . . . ??? . . . ✤ . . . ?"

You know these words.

You get your hopes up. Can it be? Iset emerges! The two of you shared a love of *patriarchy* and *power*. And yet still . . . This foreign tongue.

Note how she waves her hands, not like a priestess, but like a dancer at the Nile Flood Feast, someone who launches skyward, flipping in the air, to appease the goddess Sekhmet. And yet she does not dance.

You might even rush to her. Embrace her with the joy of a great flood. No longer will you sleep. Eternity together will be paradise, an oasis of timelessness. Now, all that remains is to complete two simple tasks:

- Kill her.   - Resurrect her.

You might not notice when the woman is trying to evade your attempt to strangle her. She'll point to herself. "Scientist," she'll say. ". . .??? 🐆??? 🗡 ???🐗. . . Oh, forget it. I'm going to say what I've always wanted to say to Brad and Kevin. Don't be a jerk. It's not that hard. DON'T. BE. A. JERK."

Jerk. This, you understand. And yet it is confounding. Iset always liked you unyielding, liked you as a "jerk."

When the 21 scribes of the Lower Kingdom threatened to revolt, she whispered hotly in your ear, "Eliminate their names." It was a fate worse than flogging to remove a man's name from his tomb.

At this point, something truly horrific might happen. This woman might come toward you, squinting at the fabric to discover where it ends and you start. Allow yourself to be disconcerted. No one has come toward you like this in millennia. Only Iset. Your subjects always prostrated themselves before you seven times and seven times, both on the belly and on the back. Take a large step backward. Do not consider it retreat. There can be no invading force, save for archaeologists. Your enemies blew away with the sands long ago.

She may even show her teeth—*a smile*. This is truly disconcerting, and it will help you remember *to switch on your Third Eye*. Good choice! The accumulated Troubleshooting Tips will now be accessible.

Troubleshooting Tip: Modern humans do not have worn-down teeth due to sand contaminating bread flour! Their teeth are enormous. They like to smile, which you may find disconcerting.

Troubleshooting Tip: Flooding is no longer the highlight of the calendar year.

Troubleshooting Tip: Average moderns often survive childhood and even young adulthood, living as long as some Pharaohs, all the way into their 60s. People in their 30s may not appear to be elders.

Troubleshooting Tip: Throughout history, artists have rendered leaders as their best selves, sinewy and beautiful, freeing leaders to enjoy diets heavy in beer, wine, bread, and honey.

Troubleshooting Tip: Throughout all time, in yesteryear as today, leaders have had diabetes.

Troubleshooting Tip: The word *gum* is derived from the ancient Egyptian word *kemai*. The moderns do not chew gum made from tree resin, however. Other words they stole from Egyptian are *oasis*, *pharaoh*, *sash*, *desert*, *Memphis*, *chemistry*, *ivory*, and the name *Susan*.

Troubleshooting Tip: No one now receives the title God's Wife of Amun-Re, so her offspring are not considered demigods from birth.

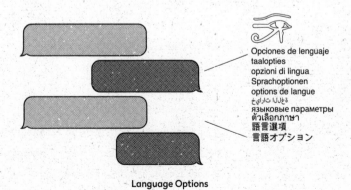

Opciones de lenguaje
taalopties
opzioni di lingua
Sprachoptionen
options de langue
خيارات اللغة
языковые параметры
ตัวเลือกภาษา
語言選項
言語オプション

Language Options

WITH YOUR NEXT generation Third Eye Security System switched on, you will now see the woman with stunning visual clarity. Pull a hand to your chest, let it nestle in your armpit and admire the quality of the image. Thanks to your Third Eye translation system, her meaning washes into your mind now, like waves on a beach.

"You're very old. . . . You probably don't know this is creepy," she says. "Can you focus on yourself instead of me?"

What might one focus on, other than oneself—the Pharaoh? Iset would never make such a remark. And they look nothing alike! Her black "hair" is a sun hat; the "smoky eye" is a pair of protective goggles, and the "beauty mark" must have been a bug (?).

"All this stress," she says. "You could have a heart attack."

Heart.

Attack.

She would curse your sacred organs?

Thanks to the Third Eye's signal extender, you can monitor other rooms in the tomb where your organs are safely stowed in Canopic jars.

Even at this distance, you'll be able to feel the rattling of the organs, vibrating an alert against the jars as clearly as if they remained in your chest. Here is the "attack" she promised to wage against your organs. But you are ready.

The woman pulls an object from her pocket, a black rectangle, followed by a writing utensil. She opens the rectangle and fans papyrus pages with her thumb. "What do you *want*? Maybe we can communicate like this," she says. She tries to hand the items to you.

FACIAL RECOGNITION

THE THIRD EYE Security System recognizes people it has seen before. It enables you to:

- Study with disdain this face that is not your wife's.
- Ensure that you see clearly her *extreme* impertinence: The Son of Sobekhotop the Brave—the Mighty Bull, He Who Makes Hearts Live—she would have him *write*? Like a scribe?

- Remove the items from her grasp before she knows what's happening.
- Throw them at the wall, safely away from yourself.
- Feel only a little remorse when your flailing arm knocks her unconscious.

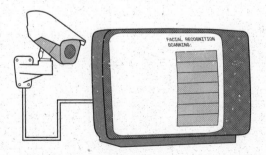

Facial Recognition Software

WITH A *QUIET* feature, the Third Eye Security System can alert you when it is time to go back to bed for a few more centuries.

Perhaps strangling more archaeologists seems preferable to sleep. You may feel tempted to switch off the system in order to enjoy the way their tendons cave in and their bodies collapse, give way to you. All you really want is that moment when their eyes search your face, seeking to know, "Father, is that you?"

However, if the Third Eye is switched off and you roam freely throughout your tomb, the intruders will likely become more adversarial, possibly even locating that magic scroll that is stored with your Canopic jars. They will recite incantations they don't even understand and annihilate you in a divine wind before you can earn your afterlife. They hate your power.

All you have to do, just for today, is stop exerting it. Retrace your steps. Leave her here, this faulty version of her that is the water's reflection of faulty you who cannot let go. Two hundred years will be tomorrow.

PERHAPS THERE IS a machine at the door trying to break it down.
The voices of men.

She presses her face to her hand, gazes at you. "Ow," she says.
Ow. It is a beautiful word. There is a spray of freckles on the nose
beneath the goggles, distant birds on a blue sky. But do not falter.
These eyes glisten, warm in the torch light, boundless. They regard
only you, in a way that no one you loved ever did. Leave her to face
accusations that she is a hysterical madwoman.

Push a revolving gold panel, steal down a passageway.

Climb into bed and crash.

Ascend to the Third Eye's secure net in the ether. Exist safely in
the Cloud until such time as you might own the sun.

(If you have trouble with your Third Eye Security System,
expect no assistance within 14 years or beyond. Upgrades are available for a cost.)

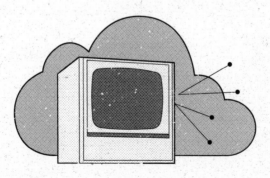

The Third Eye Cloud

THE 6 (66) HABITS OF
HIGHLY EFFECTIVE WITCHES

POWERFUL LESSONS
IN SURVIVAL MANAGEMENT

Now with
Spell Ritual
in the
Afterword!

UNAPOLOGETIC. UNSTOPPABLE. YOU were born to be a leader. People can hardly believe the loyalty you inspire, with underlings clamoring to carry out your every wish. Also, those cheekbones—while perhaps not the source of your competitive advantage, they are giving 110 percent.

Effective management is an important part of any coven or enchanted kingdom. It has always been your passion to take the knowledge and experience you have gained during a long, storied life in order to apply it to others. In all the ways that matter, you already have a largely successful enterprise.

The demand has always been there for your creativity and innovation. A skill set that includes potions, elixirs, spells, curses, and shape-shifting translates easily to multilevel income streams. After all, humans tend to have the same basic desires:

- making people fall in love with them
- traveling to usually unreachable places
- getting fabulous makeovers
- obtaining homeopathic cures for jealousy or FOMO
- predetermining the outcomes of sporting events
- to break previous spells that turned them to stone, into a toad, etc.
- overriding rules of succession in local monarchies
- candy

People are willing to pay dearly to fulfill just one of the above wishes. But you can grant them all, sometimes even simultaneously! It stands to reason that you can name your price, whether in currency, jewels, or eternal winters. People will demonize you for knowing your worth, but that comes with the territory of being a disruptor and a change agent.

While being a leader is exhilarating, it is also challenging. There aren't enough hours in the day, and no matter what anyone claims to the contrary, time cannot be managed. No spell or potion alters its uncompromising pace. You can probably respect that. Time's relentlessness is, after all, an important reason humans cherish the shortcuts you provide. However, its fleeting quality poses problems for your operations. For example, your underlings often drop dead from exhaustion, and then you have to find new ones. More importantly, though, time matures your rivals from enchanted, tragic children into peppy, meddlesome teens whose loud singing voices distract your followers, posing potential encroachment on market share.

With regard to where this organization is going, you have a vision, most likely from gazing into a crystal ball or a magic mirror. There's no way that any young upstarts or start-ups will ever interfere with your long-term objectives. . . . Is there?

Underestimating your competition is a mistake that can have serious consequences. Most notably, you may leave your vulnerabilities exposed. A shrewd rival will capitalize on your underestimation, quietly setting plans in motion to acquire new territory in the background. For example, let's say you are water-soluble. By the time you notice the offensive presence and attempt to dislodge it, your competitor may already have taken advantage of the buckets of water you keep around the castle, dousing you and procuring your broom, not to mention humiliating your smartly dressed team of flying monkeys. At that point, it's too late.

There are leadership clichés that everyone knows, such as:

- The secret to success is to know something no one else knows.
- Appeal to people's self-interest, not their compassion or gratitude.
- Use the right posture for leadership (stooped or unnaturally erect).
- Keep people dependent on you.
- Don't lead by example.

- It's better to demand forgiveness than to ask permission.
- Surround yourself with yes-men.
- Everything you want is on the other side of human fear.
- Someone is sitting in the shade today because someone planted a tree a long time ago. (Question: Why is some jackhole under your tree?)

If you are facing a hostile takeover, you will need to get beyond these obvious platitudes. Internalize a few key survival tips and you might avoid falling into the (fiery) red. It's worth a try.

TIP 1:
As a Female Leader, Don't Be Proactive

IN THE EVENT that your competitor is unconscious in a glass coffin, her proxy may be a prince, sometimes accompanied by a hunting party comprising vague, anonymous men or, less often, men with names. Comfort and disarm these fellows with the following strategies. With a bit of luck, they will undervalue your contributions, rather than kill you.

- Although you are the boss, be less *bossy*.
- Offer beatific smiles and a neutral gaze. No *crazy eyes*, no squinting, no blue eye shadow.
- Be just a little bit confident—the right amount, shy of mousy.
- Pretend to have Imposter Syndrome.
- Let everyone finish their dumb remarks, repressing the urge to shout, *Silence!*
- On your annual review, list your strengths as *organized, team player,* and *enthusiastic.*
- Leave the high-collar cape at home and wear a cardigan twin set instead.
- To throw them off the trail, say, whenever possible, *This is a witch hunt!*
- Feel bad about characterizing reserved women leaders as "mousy," even if only in your thoughts, but still strive not to be like that and then feel bad about that, as well.
- Be the only person in the room concerned with perceptions of female leaders.
- Don't laugh with your mouth open.
- Don't shoot lightning out of your wand. Practice waving it daintily.
- *Absolutely no flawless, arched brows.*

TIP 2:
End with the
Beginning in Mind

HUMANS WILL TRANSGRESS. That's what they do. They will trespass onto your property. They will renege on the deals they have made in writing, even ones signed in blood. They'll kill your sister and steal her shoes. They'll crawl onto the roof of the gingerbread house where you live and *eat* it. They will invite everyone in the whole town to their royal baby's christening except for you. They will steal vegetables from the magical garden you lovingly cultivated. The list goes on and on. There's seemingly no end to how rude they can be. In matters of business, they say to "begin with the end in mind," but you weren't the one who began any of this.

TIP 3:
Banish the "Win-Win" Paradox

IT IS UNDERSTANDABLE to feel frustrated. Even though ambition is motivating, it can be messy. If you do whatever it takes to win, such as morph into your other form, they'll perceive you as a *monster*. Your rival will have forced you off-brand. In the event that you are not stabbed or impaled, it may take years to rebuild your messaging.

Conventional wisdom says that, instead of repressing and stewing over emotions, great leaders own them. A simple statement— even something as simple as *I feel angry*—is supposed to make you relatable. However, coming from you, a statement like *I feel angry* won't be tolerated. When they tell the story later, they'll say you were unstable, hysterical, or that there was "just something they didn't like" about your pantsuit. They may even claim that you turned into a huge black dragon or a sea serpent. Maybe you did and maybe you didn't. But the point is that people will believe them. If you don't stand up for yourself, you are a patsy. If you do, you're a monster. In this regard, there is no winning. You might as well please yourself.

TIP 4:
Synergize

WHILE IT MAY seem rational to spare younger women all the non-sense you've endured by locking them into towers until the dawn of a better era, there are times when working with these potential rivals—*co-opetition*—makes good business sense. Rather than clinging to a zero-sum game, consider changing the rules. Humans do it all the time. Plus, it could be fun to take on a protégé. The next time you climb up your ward's long hair to inspect the lock on her chastity belt, test the waters by engaging in some activities designed to explore your potential as a team.

An easy option is creating a vision board together. What should you put on your vision board? Anything you want!

To get started, generate some clear, measurable goals. For example, your joint venture might involve devising recipes for new remedies. Compose a list of common deformities you might work together to cure:

- Alto or tenor singing voice
- Homeliness
- Having a noticeable nose
- Being a mermaid
- Aging

Here are some suggested supplies to have on hand:

- Markers
- Cardboard
- Glue sticks
- Wrapping paper
- Deadly nightshade
- Animal tongues
- Glitter
- Peacock feathers
- Willow bark
- Dead man's toes
- Ribbons
- Hemlock

If you're willing to venture out of the tower, you may get a better sense of the potential for this partnership. The activities below provide flexible objectives, allowing for quick pivots. You'll be able to execute a cost-benefit analysis. If you find that this union is not a good fit or if you can't maintain leverage or if it just isn't fun, you can simply omit the analysis and focus on the *execution*.

ACTIVITY	PARTNERSHIP DISSOLUTION PLAN
Trust fall	Ravine
Ropes course	Alligators
Group juice cleanse	Poisoned apple add-ins
Paintball	Fireball
Dinner-dance or disco	Fatal blisters

TIP 5:
Seek to Be Understood Rather than to Understand

GIVEN HOW HUMANS interact with one another, what are the chances that you can reach an understanding with them? For example, humans sometimes berate fellow humans on whom their very survival may depend, even in spite of the fact that *they cannot put spells on anyone*. Almost daily, people behave badly toward the individuals serving their food or driving the vehicles that hurtle them wildly through space to Whole Foods. Let's not even get started about the behavior directed at nurses, a group with skills that include setting up IV bags and administering medicines through them that travel straight into the human body.

Trying to understand humans could lead to a confusion spiral from which you might not escape. As such, do not try to meet humans *where they are*, as the conventional wisdom suggests, because they might be in a dark, small place with a recliner and a 24-hour news channel. They might be yelling long-winded monologues that resemble incantations. Even though there's no power behind these "spells," you'll end up there for hours on a leather sofa saying, "Uh-huh" and "I'm going to head out now. . . ." You'll think you can just tiptoe out of there, but somehow it won't be that easy.

Instead, increase the odds of survival by adhering to these (far more) simple guidelines:

- Avoid hallowed ground.
- Steer clear of sentient woodland creatures or anyone shorter than waist height.
- Try to curse an object that is more imposing than a spindle.
- Change your name from Grimhilde to Katy or Jordan.
- Do not join a coven of "mean girl" witches.
- Give a wide berth to that large oven you use for cooking children.
- Don't cook children, even though they are succulent and obnoxious.
- Go blond (see more on this below).

TIP 6:
Dull the Saw

IN BUSINESS, THE common wisdom is to "sharpen the saw." But your sharp saw is the whole problem in the first place. If push comes to shove and your survival is at stake, *dull* the saw. You are too old to be a bride and too young to be a grandmother. This is off-putting to humans. Whether you reside in *Smoke Town* or *Old Hagville*, you must stop being a middle-aged woman at the intersection of *Ambitious* and *Unmarried*. They think your marital status and success justify eating your roof.

Below are some (lesser) versions of you that humans will tolerate a bit better:

DOMESTIC WITCH (TYPICALLY BLOND):
Whether you live in a bottle or sleep in a twin bed, you'll use your powers to starch your husband's shirts and to boost his career prospects in the military or advertising. Mind-numbing, yes, but safe. Alternatively, if marriage isn't for you, become a magical, unpaid governess. This position offers an interesting challenge because you must elicit from children the adoration normally reserved for a super-cool teen sister, as well as the respect appropriate for a prison warden.

CUTE, PREPUBESCENT WITCH (TYPICALLY BLOND):
This is easy work—you'll be whip smart (which you already are) and say pithy one-liners (which you already do). The hard part won't be learning about the active chemical compounds in crocodile dung, drams of fat, toad venom, or wombs of the hare. It will be your relegation to a supporting role (see also "Grandmotherly/blue-hair").

GRANDMOTHERLY/BLUE-HAIR:

You will make outfits for other people, convey uplifting aphorisms, and turn dishonest puppets into real boys. It's a total nightmare, your version of living in the suburbs, complete with the risk of bored, self-combustion. What's worse, you will have a button nose. Bibbetty-Bobbetty Boop!

CHEEKY/REVENGE WITCH:

With abilities more reminiscent of celebrity chefs than supernatural entities, you and two brassy roommates will make potions from instructions in a book you found, the recipes tailored toward humiliation of your ex-husbands. Toupees and underpants will fly! Those 20-something girlfriends will dump them! It'll be really great.

Conclusion

NO MATTER WHERE you are in life, you can live by the 6(66) habits. Develop routines of self-discipline and perform acts of self-love every day, such as a morning exercise routine that includes trying out new spells on your pet cat, crow, frog, or owl. An evening herbal bath is not only relaxing, but it also has the added benefit of making it impossible for anyone to burn you to death. Consider the below recipe. Can you devise others?

DIRECTIONS

Combine:

Lavender

Honey

Water buffalo tooth

Eyelashes

Ground turtle shell

Graveyard dirt

Boil this potion, removing scum from the surface. Rub on your face.

DOSAGE: Dollop the size of a big toe

INCANTATION:
Upon going to sleep, say the following after you have eaten ritually pure food:

"Verily by Neith, verily by Neith, if I shall succeed in business, show me water, if not, fire. I adjure you by the God of the Gods, drag, smite, cause to fall all rivals . . . or at least allow me to make some coin curing hemorrhoids and wet coughs."

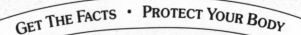

"WHAT'S HAPPENING TO MY BODY?"

Radioactive Mutants and the Safety of the Nuclear Family

THE CHANGES AHEAD!

HEY, GUESS WHAT? You have a body, a wonderful body, and it's *changing*.

This special time of growth began when you drove through an atomic cloud or camped on top of a nuclear waste dump, and it will end when your body has reached its new shape and size. During this transformation, you'll likely grow up and out, and not all parts will grow at the same pace. You may, at times, look and feel like an awkward, clumsy puppy! This will be especially true on the day that your genitals either become wildly aggressive, complete with unwanted humping, or they disappear entirely. You'll also notice changes in your skin, fingernails, and appetite. There will be bumps where you used to be flat, and you will be smooth where you used to have hair.

New emotions are coming your way, too, which might lead to unfamiliar dynamics in your relationships or could spur you to develop interests you never had in the past. All of these changes are caused by *radiation*, the energy particles that help you to blossom and mushroom into the new you. No action needed! It's sort of awesome how you can sit back as your body transforms itself.

However, take note that this can also be a time of great vulnerability. Your body affects the choices you make with your mind. What accounts for the dangers you may face? Cell degradation!

Signs of cellular degradation include:

- Headaches
- Visible somatic mutations
- Increased drive for dramatic sensations
- Kidnapping people
- Decreased concern about making mistakes

- Inability to envision a few minutes into the future
- Dozing off in the middle of staring menacingly at someone
- Being overcome with giggles that won't let up

Sometimes, bad actors will try to take advantage of your new situation in order to pressure you into perilous enterprises like hand-to-hand combat. At other times, these bad influences might criticize you in public for your new appearance with voices so shrill that your self-esteem and your eardrums simply vanish. Serious consequences can result from allowing yourself to be lured away from the support system of your nuclear family, such as perishing before you get the chance to expire from radiation poisoning or, worse yet, failing to gain admittance to the college of your choice. Below are tips for navigating a confusing world that seems at once familiar and brand-new.

CELEBRATE THE UNIQUE YOU!

YOU'RE ONE OF a kind, beautiful in your own unique way. Yet, it is only natural to have some questions, such as *Why is everyone screaming?*

Remember that your body is a work in progress. Try not to focus on what it looks like. Instead, think about all the great things your body can do.

For example, note how, when you're ready, you can emerge from the sea and scoop up teen girls in bikinis, all the while fending off their hunky boyfriends and avoiding lacerations from heavily sprayed 1960s coiffures. Wow! That's pretty impressive.

You don't need to measure yourself against anyone at all, including radioactive friends or family who may now live in a cave with you or in a major city's sewers. These changes are not a race. There are no prizes for being the first to lose your toenails or to grow a new row of baby teeth.

To have a positive attitude, try to see yourself as others might, the way your inner light makes you shine. You have a luminous glow, especially in your eyes when it's dark outside. Refuse to hunt for negative aspects of yourself or for large, male humans. The little ones are less dangerous and easier to catch.

LISTEN UP!

YOUR BODY IS talking to you. Can you hear it? Tune into your body and hear its warnings. If your body says it's sleepy, hit the hay early. If your body is thirsty, drink more neon green groundwater.

It's especially important to be a healthy eater at this time. Your *outsides* and your *insides* are more interconnected all the time. Your body needs sustenance to maintain its transformation so you can continue to exist and to prowl. Oozing burns a lot of calories.

Do you ever really want or crave something? You don't know why you want this thing. You just want it. This is called *cannibalistic desire*, and it's different from wanting ice cream or wanting someone to be your best friend or wanting to snuggle with the nest of snakes in your cave. It is also different from the homicidal urges that you may experience at times.

Cannibalistic desire means that you feel very attracted to someone in a strong way. Someone like you. The attraction is like the force from a nuclear reactor—the way it draws you close, evoking the irresistible urge to wrap your lips around the centrifuge to suck out more energy.

If your body is hungry, it can be hard to ignore it. Understandably, you will wish to take a leisurely hike through the mountain pass to the gas station minimart, where you can grab a family of vacationers and a bag of Combos.

Take note, however: Your body is yours and yours alone. You have the right to protect it from anyone—rogue family member, friend, or person you're consuming. If anyone punches or scratches you when you try to eat them, tell the rest of your nuclear family. Never keep it secret that you've adopted a humanitarian diet or that you've brought home takeout. There's safety in numbers, especially atomic numbers over 92.

If you notice that anyone has watched your activities, let your family know. Did some nosy human lurk nearby when you snagged your lunch? Lurkers and busybodies must be dealt with very decisively. Your family must be informed in order to support you in this endeavor. Left unaddressed, humans with ill intent will recruit others, and these bullies can become quite ugly indeed.

SOME PEOPLE HAVE NOTICED A BAD SMELL. WHAT TO DO?

AT SOME POINT, you might notice hair sprouting in strange places, such as your gums. This hair might not match the color and texture of the hair on your liver or in your esophagus. Along with this change, it's possible that everything about you smells bad, with the notable exception of your armpits. Unfortunately, this slimy scent trail makes it easy for the police or survivors of the family you've been eating to find you. Take control of your body by taking care of it. The shrinking number of cells in your mucous membranes makes this more important than ever.

HEALTHY HABITS

CHANGE CAN BE exciting but it can also be a little confusing. Every hour, it seems, you grow bigger and stronger, gain weight, and change color. Your arms, legs, and frontal lobe are developing new proportions. Clothes that once suited you are too tight, too short, and too intact. Even your facial features are changing!

Create a personal hygiene routine! Your safety and well-being may depend on it.

At least weekly:

- Sharpen your remaining teeth and fingernails.
- Wipe away bone marrow leaks or other fluids.
- Comb excess skin bacteria into tidy braids or a topknot.
- Dry and polish exposed areas of your spinal column.

A few times a month:

- Floss the tendons or other gristle from your teeth.
- Shampoo your oral areas.
- Oil your bondage gear—spiked harness, spiked headwear, spiked choker, etc.

INTERNAL CHANGES

THERE'S SO MUCH going on with your body that you might forget to take note of your head and heart. You might start to think and feel differently about your old friends, classmates, and drifters who pass through town. As you transform, you're also likely to take less interest in what people think of you—or possibly even no interest at all. You may notice that you're angry or annoyed more often or that things bother you that didn't bother you before. Sometimes you may turn to your radioactive "family" for support, while at other times you will turn to them with an axe, disdain, or a poisonous snake.

THE PROBLEMS WITH GETTING INTO A DRAMA

DRAMA IS CRISIS. It is all-consuming, draining everything you have and more. You may not sleep. You may not stop to eat, not even if there's a relatively fresh corpse nearby. When you're in a drama, you're so full of feelings—irritation, frustration, rage—that everything seems black and white. It's as if there's only one way forward, whether it's setting upon a car with a flat tire, breaking into a stranger's home, or incinerating someone you used to know. However, if you have trouble destroying a person with your (normally) combustible embrace, pause for a moment. Take a step back. Maybe two steps. Have you drained yourself of energy? This is why you should not alienate your family. They will always be there to finish off the lady beating you with a lamp or the well-intentioned, but misguided professor with a Geiger counter.

STRESS!

STRESS MAKES YOU very uncomfortable, as does the collapse of your central nervous system. It's true that there are circumstances outside your control, everything from limb tremors to booby traps people have set for you. And due to the delirium caused by cerebral syndrome, it's also true that you can't control your mind. Exercises that *won't* work as you navigate all these changes include:

- Doing a sitting meditation
- Making up a gratitude list
- Observing a leaf for five minutes
- Speaking in sentences
- Eating a raisin mindfully

The good news is that there are some exercises that *are* appropriate for this pivotal time in your life.

REFLECTIVE EXERCISES

❑ **OBSERVING OTHER PEOPLE–** You can practice this from anywhere, a cliff ledge or a rooftop or a subway tunnel. Although you might feel the urge to stare at one particular person, probably someone under 20, and watch what she is doing 24 hours a day, it would be safer to spread your attention around. Watch a tai chi class in the park or the old guys playing chess. *From afar.*

❑ **THE BODY SCAN–** Your binoculars can be great fun. It's true that they allow you to scan your favorite subject's head, shoulders, neck, chest, legs, chest, chest, legs, and chest. However, anytime the binoculars are in use, you are unaware of the immediate surroundings. Take a moment to put them down, breathe the fresh air, and take note of each part of you. How do you feel? Scan each body part periodically for knife or axe handles.

❑ **THE MINDFUL WINDOW–** Distance affects perspective. Perhaps for a better view, you have approached a window and stared into it, working hard to observe shapes, colors, textures, and nipples. The action inside the house is so exciting that you could forget about the action behind you. Pause. Be mindful of your environment. Have you ever found yourself in the headlights of a big brother's pickup truck or a police car?

❑ **PAYING ATTENTION TO MUSIC–** Listening to music is not only enjoyable, but it changes your brain waves. Take a moment to identify the song that's playing. What are the lead instruments? Do you hear a tuba emitting an ominous F or F sharp? This exciting tune may indicate the opportunity to make your move, but it might also indicate that someone else has made a move and is about to bludgeon you with a lawn ornament.

MINDFUL EATING– When you see people being eaten around you, perhaps you feel the urge to eat them, too. Mindful eating involves awareness of your relationship with food. You've already done a great job of savoring the smell and appearance of the person you plan to eat. However, if you're about to grab someone in between meals, ask yourself: *Am I really hungry? Or am I simply worried that my family member will eat this babysitter before I do?*

If you do eat her, don't just grunt and swallow. Take small bites. Taste and chew instead of gnawing in a frenzy. Chewing will help you feel fuller longer, maybe up to several minutes longer. Plus, if you eat slowly, you may take notice of the loved ones of the person you're eating, who are about to impale you with the car antenna from their station wagon.

ACTIVE EXERCISES

REGARDLESS OF YOUR phase of degeneration, a "play break" can have serious benefits, keeping your blood pressure as low as 240/90, a level that may help you evade the angry people whose relatives you just ate. Accordingly, a play break improves the odds that you may get to die from natural causes, such as inflammation of the heart sac, diffusion of subcutaneous tissues, or a perforated bowel.

Research has linked endeavors like the ones below to decreased mortality from human aggression, one's own mistakes, or other unnatural causes.

- ❏ **DO A MAGIC TRICK–** Instead of kidnapping a baby, drape a black cloth over that succulent nugget and shout *Presto!* The enchanted audience will be transfixed, rather than upset, by the disappearance and they'll chatter about how the trick was performed instead of tracking you to the cave or subway system where you live.
- ❏ **BUILD SOMETHING FUN,** such as a lockable storage trunk for your stockpile of pickaxes, swords, and explosives. Later, you'll enjoy hours of entertainment not being attacked by trespassers wielding your own weapons.
- ❏ **TRY DIFFERENT "SLIME" RECIPES WITH GLITTER** to throw pursuers off your own slime trail.

- ❏ **RESEARCH NEW WAYS TO WHISTLE–** using a blade of grass, your thumbs, or a frequency only dogs can hear. Summon aggressive German shepherds that would otherwise surprise you later. It's very enjoyable to maul rather than to be mauled!
- ❏ **CLIMB A TREE–** But wait! While you're there, Do NOT nail a random person to it and set it ablaze, regardless of how crispy and yummy you know that person will turn out. Instead, consider throwing the traitorous member of your family out of it.

FINAL WORDS

BE PROUD. YOU have shown yourself capable of tackling so much—not only a new subterranean life, but also the citizens you've met during your travels. While there are a lot of twists and turns on the desert road or subway system ahead, they're all leading someplace phenomenal. Congratulations!

JOURNAL PAGE!

You're going through some big changes right now, both internal and external. Take a moment to reflect on how you are today, compared to one day ago. Write about the transformations that have taken place in your body and mind:

My chromosomal aberrations: _____

_____

_____

_____

My relationships: _____

_____

_____

_____

My nose: _____

_____

_____

_____

My forehead: _____

_____

_____

_____

My interests: _____

_____

_____

_____

_____

My home in the cave/sewer: _____

_____

_____

_____

_____

Changes I'm waiting for: _____

_____

_____

_____

_____

How I feel about these changes: _____

_____

_____

_____

_____

USA! USA!

Exceptionally Large Beings and the Unanticipated Stress of Acknowledgment

(Large Print Edition)

YOU DIDN'T CHOOSE this life, the way crowds gather when you're spotted in public. You have become a recluse for a reason. Basic activities that most take for granted attract gawkers and paparazzi, even endeavors such as a quick bite or a sojourn through the misty forest or inlet where you live.

It's not just that you draw attention because you eclipse things. You also have that X-factor that excites people and motivates them to take action. What is it about you? Charisma is difficult to quantify, as is your height or length. But in any case, you inspire folks and get them talking. They are breathless with conjecture: What is the source of your outsize energy? Why does your island or nest remain uncharted territory, unlisted on maps to the stars? How can ordinary people get a piece of you?

While your status bestows certain freedoms, such as high-speed travel and the luxury to dine wherever you please without a wait, the liberties of anonymity can quickly recede. Regard your unique prominence as a good thing that needs to be monitored and kept in check.

You do face challenges, but remember that no one wants to hear your complaints. *Ooh. I'm so exceptionally big and strong. Woe is me.* And yet it's true that you can't do simple things the Average Joe can do, such as go out and ride a bicycle. This is partly because your legs are too long or because you have too few legs or too many, but mostly it's because of the potential to be mobbed. The resultant isolation is hard. You're bored. So, you eat more. And then you get *even bigger and stronger*. It's a vicious circle that could land you in a vicious circus.

People think you are living the dream—or possibly that you are living within *their* dream/nightmare—and they are upset that they can't tell for sure. They may want to poke you to see if you are real. As such, being a celebrity can attract stalkers. You may be harassed by phone, email, or inappropriate DMs. A follower's obsession can turn into threats, possibly ones that involve camping in your backyard. Therefore, another consequence of your high profile is that you are always a potential target for kidnapping and violence.

Handle your magnificent stature responsibly and with care. If you don't, it can quickly get the better of you.

Shrug Off Gossip

GOSSIPS ARE RELENTLESS at trying to unearth your personal information, especially your address. They pore over every detail that's known about your private life in hopes of pinpointing your latitude and longitude. These speculations can inspire frenzies in the populace that result in pursuits of anyone who even remotely resembles you. Expect constant rumors about your comings and goings, often wildly contradictory, such as simultaneous claims that you "never existed" and that you "are extinct" (typically since the Prehistoric, Ice, or Bronze Age).

Once you are solidly in the limelight, though, expect to be judged. Tabloids, magazines, newspapers, blogs, and other media voices assess everything about you—your personality, your habits, your activities, your relationships, your tail (or lack thereof), and so forth. The pictures are guaranteed to be awful, featuring just your close-up blurry eye or a distant image of you wearing an unflattering expression while you swat away whatever's making you itchy, such as machine gun bullets. But the worst part is that it can be demeaning to read nasty, insulting, and derogatory lies about yourself. A million people are talking behind your back at any given time, often making you the butt of jokes, sometimes including jokes about your butt if you have one because it's so "big." Never mind the fact that it wouldn't make sense for your butt to be anything other than big. Don't expect logic. They would make rude comments if your butt were small, as well.

Learn not to take criticism personally. Resist the urge to Google yourself. But if you do, understand that people will project onto you the insecurities they have about themselves. Accept that radically different opinions will exist about your character. Some will call you a *monster*, while others will argue until their dying breath that you are a *beast*, a *behemoth*, a *leviathan*, a *colossus*, or a *titan*. Cultivate acceptance by laughing off criticism. In addition to helping you cope with the situation, this approach will be objectively terrifying. This strategy may ward off people, allowing you to swim or rampage away from the situation.

Embrace the Voice That Comes with Your Position

BECAUSE THERE ARE many eyes on you, you can motivate your followers to accomplish things. Take advantage of your star power to draw attention to causes you feel strongly about, such as *being left alone*. You need to communicate to others your intentions so that they understand where you are coming from. It is vital that your followers know where you stand, which is likely on a mountain or an island that is named for you, something that should have been a clue to them in the first place that it is yours, not theirs. To communicate your passion on this topic effectively, you will need to pluck up the courage to roar about it. It is also helpful if you can get up the nerve to reveal something about yourself that might surprise your followers, such as your teeth.

Coping with the Fishbowl

LIFE IS NOT simple when you are continuously growing, especially when it's happening in the public eye or near a public beach. One day, after the simple meal of a lonely teen swimmer, you're suddenly flush with notoriety and you find yourself recognized instantly whenever and wherever you come up for air. Sought after by thousands, you're made to feel important and wanted. You receive invitations to the most exclusive gatherings—so exclusive that you're the only guest sometimes. When you arrive, people scream. There might even be cage dancers waving their arms at you, often extending exciting cuts of meat or sparkly flares. These are indeed coveted prizes, especially the arms.

But the scary downside to fame eats into the lives of many. People generally expect more from you when you are a high-profile individual. You are expected to be absolutely perfect every single moment of the day. Such an expectation is impossible to meet, of course. Nevertheless, when you are reported as having done something wrong, such as daring to lunch in public and actually eat, you will be highly scrutinized. If the offense is small—for example, the consumption of a family pet or a tax lawyer—you may be able to work your way back into others' good graces with the help of a PR firm. However, if the offense is significant and if you also chew with your mouth open, smacking your food so everyone can see it, you may never get people to turn their backs on you forever, as you'd hoped.

What's more, paparazzi have little respect for your privacy. They will chase you—hiding, lying in wait, and even disguising themselves as sides of beef, just to take that elusive shot. There are numerous tragic examples of paparazzi aggression toward targets, resulting in high-speed pursuits with terrible consequences, like hit-and-run boat crashes and exploding oxygen tanks down the gullet. *People* once declared paparazzi "the least sexy group alive." Unfortunately for you, they are indeed alive. Even if you pick off a few, there will soon be new ones. No one really understands their life cycle.

Place Value on Existing Relationships

REMEMBER TO NURTURE your inner circle, if you have one. For example, retain close contact with the remote tribe that lives down the way. Long-standing relationships are important for keeping you unaffected. The real you is a normal individual, vulnerable as anyone else to time, destiny, and the men who intend to gas you unconscious and load you onto a ship headed to New York.

Your high-visibility status may put close relationships to the test, and this is something you should be prepared for. Spend time having one-on-one conversations with the chief, explaining your goals, values, and intentions. Express that, in exchange for keeping the tribe safe from anachronistic dinosaurs on the island, he does not need to provide an offering—certainly not a "golden woman" (i.e., a blond bombshell) he abducted from the aforementioned ship. You'd be happy with a coffee cake or a simple *Thank you*.

Beware of New Relationships

AT TIMES, THE pressures of fame will get to you. Let's say the performance schedule of your new one-man show, "The Eighth Wonder of the World," has been beyond grueling, and you just want to break your chains, blow off some steam. You're a newcomer, and the only person in all of New York City who has been a little bit nice to you is the golden woman—who, again, you didn't kidnap, but were *offered*. So, you very understandably go to her place to take her out for a night on the town. There is nothing wrong with reaching out to others when it comes to dealing with the pressures of fame, even if you must do so through her open window.

However, be on the lookout for opportunists. There will always be those who, like the golden woman, stay by your side only until they get what they want, which might be *to not be eaten* or *to be let go*. Sincere companions will become a rarity. Opportunists are those who seek a relationship in order to escape from you or in order to gain access to your internal organs. If someone you don't know asks you to step toward a large hole covered with palm fronds, proceed with caution.

Keep a strong, responsible grip on your finances and the spires of any skyscrapers you ascend. An awareness of your situation may enable you to make smart decisions about commitments you want to enter and don't want to enter. There are arrangements you cannot afford to accept, such as one-handed dogfights with fighter jets, especially if the golden woman is clutched in the one free hand you might use to defend yourself. Don't feel bad about dropping people who were never really your friends in the first place.

Take Extra Care with Your Neonates

LET'S SAY YOU are a big, tough anaconda. If you find it overwhelming to handle the pressures of celebrity, just imagine what it's like for your hatchlings, who are trying to molt in these circumstances. You should expect zero respect for personal or family boundaries from sycophants. These people will think nothing of barging right into your den and approaching your knot of babies. It is of paramount importance that sires/guardians help their spawn to maintain balance. Here's how:

- Provide a nest that exudes warmth, happiness, and predictable odors or textures.
- Design a security system that reassures the hatchlings. This might include establishing a thick, private curtain of cobwebs or booby traps.
- Help the hatchlings understand that they are demigods so that they grow up normal and successful.
- Pay special attention to anyone who knocks and announces themselves as "JLo and Ice Cube."

- Do not miss out on regular exercise, whenever possible—stalking, hunting, striking, ambushing, submersion, beheading, and calisthenics.
- If a boat full of trophy hunters shows up, consider a vacation to unwind as a family at an easy, all-inclusive resort like Sandals.

Address Followers with Care

IT'S ALL TOO easy to have a negative impact on your image with just one misstep, especially if you are a giant crab with telepathic powers. Just because you can "speak" in the voices of those you've eaten because you absorb their consciousnesses, it doesn't mean that you should. Take a minute or two to gauge whether this is the proper time or place. Could your newest group of followers be put off by this? Consider whether they're distracted because you seem full of yourself, and also full of the missing scientists they came here to rescue. Your followers may be more respectful of your private time if you do not provide this particular kind of openness when in public.

- When you "talk" to followers IRL, think about your image and how you're holding your pinschers. Try to share in the excitement of the moment together, especially the moment with the lady scientist in the swimsuit. Be gracious about posing for photos.
- When responding to comments on social media, keep replies brief and cheery. If someone else handles this responsibility for you, make sure that they are maintaining a telepathic voice that you would actually use. By avoiding controversial statements, you give people no reason to discuss your many personalities.
- Accept your responsibility. Being a prominent figure means you can influence people in a serious way. This can be an overwhelming obligation because you have so much to juggle. While it's important to keep in mind your goal of reaching the mainland in order to subsume more minds and inflate your ego, you must also try to think outside of yourself because outside of yourself is where you'll lay your eggs.

Consider the Collective

LET'S FACE IT—WE'RE looking at an "us" versus "Them!" situation. Cultivate relationships with those who have your welfare at heart, and those whose welfare matters to you, as well. For example, consider fortifying your connection with the other giant ants in your colony, if you belong to one. Beware, though, that if all of you soak in the attention, you may collectively delude yourselves into believing the hype. Maybe you *are* the ultimate emblem of threats ushered in by the Atomic Age. However, believing your own press may lead to exponentially riskier behaviors than you might undertake otherwise. The next thing you know, you have become a member of a "Brat Pack," wantonly pilfering sugar from the rail yard or relocating your nest within the hull of a *fully armed* naval ship. Such reckless, self-indulgent folly can lead to embarrassing mug shots in the news media that may haunt you forever. Instead, get involved in selfless voluntary community service, such as sacrificing yourself to the flamethrowers so that the Queen may escape and continue to lay eggs in the sewers.

Keep Up Healthy Habits

IF YOU HAVE just recently become famous, you might be overwhelmed by your new visibility. This will be true whether you are an intelligent leech, a Gila monster, a shrew, a tarantula, a wasp, or something else entirely. Try to keep up your regular routines, such as eating cattle and hoboes. Change your routines only when they need to be changed (according to new feeding needs or new assailants). Continue using healthy outlets for stress, like spending time alone, resting, exercising, and preying mainly on the "immoral" people in the nearby town. This will keep you stable when life feels chaotic.

- When you are unable to keep up these habits, there is a much higher risk of getting swept up in the negative possibilities of fame, like having too much cosmetic surgery, making self-righteous speeches at awards shows, and dressing "Bo-ho."
- Set boundaries for yourself. Because of the high demands of fame, you will find yourself needing to

say no. Make clear how long you will take questions and gunfire. By hopping over a building or a fort, you can set the agenda, and others will follow suit. This is much better than not making your plans clear and then having to sidestep awkward followers who are literally in your way.

- Remember that you are never obligated to answer questions about your personal life or to respond to bazookas and missiles, and some high-profile figures make it a rule not to. To do so would be to "let them see you sweat"—something you want to avoid in the absence of sweat glands.

Conclusion

HAVING A HIGH profile often comes with a heavy price, typically involving explosions or falling a long way. Individuals who are in the spotlight or searchlight have the same problems as regular people and they will make mistakes. The important thing is to do what is best for your own life and not worry about how to please everyone else, as this would be a form of belittling yourself. Don't succumb to the pressure *be little,* as this would change you fundamentally. Always remain true to your values and beliefs and size. If people see that you are changeable, then they will not take you seriously. Be consistent. This will reduce any future misunderstandings without the need to reduce yourself.

THE
BENEFITS OF
COLLABORATIVE
CONSUMPTION

A New

Employee Handbook

for Swarms, Flocks, Schools,
Droves, Broods, Colonies,
Murders, and Hordes

ISSUED TO

Bioweapon Coalescensce Center

Section 51 Viaduct

17103

Welcome!

WELCOME TO YOUR new swarm, flock, school, drove, brood, colony, murder, or horde. If you have the drive to explore an egalitarian lifestyle—within avian, piscine, arachnid, or other like-minded species groups—you are in the right place. This venerable organization has been in business ever since it was designed as a bioweapon for the Vietnam War. Or, possibly, it was founded in response to being gassed by agribusinesses. It's possible that no one remembers the circumstances of its founding.

In any case, the overriding goal of the outfit is *to get all over everything*. Its mission of *becoming unstoppable* is not a foregone conclusion, but it does have about an 80 percent chance of coming to fruition.

A group is only as successful as its commitment not to concern itself with individuals. It is crucial to learn to function as one unrelenting unit. By adhering to the guidelines here, you can help to ensure that this organization remains unified. Failure to do so may result in mass extermination or getting sucked into a jet engine.

1 Introduction:
Signing the Social Contract

YOUR INTEREST IN this organization does, in itself, suggest that you are a good fit for helping fulfill the mission. In fact, you may already have been drawn to the excitement like a gravitational pull, almost against your will. If so, congratulations! If not, don't despair. Strive to swim or fly a little faster. Alternatively, wait in some greenery for the group to loop in your direction.

Being a valuable team member can facilitate new opportunities because your colleagues will see for themselves your stellar performances in tackling low-stakes nighttime projects, such as ravaging the town wino or some skinny-dipping teens. If you build on that success by eating more than your share of "the only scientist around here who knows about us," perhaps you'll be invited to apply your strengths to a higher-profile endeavor, like ingesting a search party in the daytime. Eventually, you may even get a turn pecking Tippy Hedren. This is why learning to be a reliable team player is so important. If you make a big impression, especially on tougher sinewy areas, the sky is truly the only limit.

1.1 Changes in policy

THIS HANDBOOK REPLACES previous employee handbooks, memos, and manuals. The organization reserves the right to poop or puke with or without notice, on all or any part of this handbook. Employees are unlikely to be notified of changes.

1.2 Mission

IN SHORT, THE mission is to eat. But whom shall you eat? And when?

Human worker drones can often be found doing *side hustles*, typically waiting tables on outdoor patios at TGIFridays or teaching swimming at local camps. However, although these workers are readily available and have amazing calf muscles, your organization has astutely discerned that it can avoid military-grade bombs or flamethrowers by applying its efforts toward *the rich*, whom no one likes.

For humans, the term *collaborative consumption* is connected to the concept of *sharing*, whether the items "shared" are cars, apartments, power tools, or other assets. How it works is that humans pay a third party, generally a *company* founded by a well-heeled person named Evan or Kevin, in order to rent out their items in exchange for a percentage of the profits. As in most profiteering business models, the third party in the situation makes out better than the other parties. As such, people resent CEOs and secretly wish they'd be eaten.

Given these factors, some of the aims implicit in the mission include:

- When first appearing on a private island or in an exclusive neighborhood, gather in groups that could *almost* be mistaken for normal-sized swarms, flocks, schools, droves, broods, colonies, murders, or hordes, so that no one calls the police.
- Be a little agitated and buzzy, splashy, flappy, hoppy, or squawky so that the solitary, wealthy person squints inquisitively. Then simmer down in order make the person doubt his perceptions, which he will indicate by removing his glasses and rubbing his forehead.
- Gather in a showy way (such as atop wrought-iron gates and ornate window ledges) to remind the rich person that the trappings of wealth will provide no defenses. Not this time.
- Obviously, you can then go ahead and pluck out the eyes of people perceived as deserving of a good eye-pluck, such as bored socialites, arrogant lawyers, and especially those *fat cats* responsible for pesticides.
- Pick off these people one by one. The rich spend time by themselves in capacious areas that could fit a million percent more individuals in them. No one will notice. In fact, when Brad, the tennis instructor, comes on Tuesday, he will think absolutely nothing of it when no one answers the door. He'll presume the resident is having an episode endemic to the wealthy called *a mood* or *the vapors*, and he'll simply drive away again in his Yaris.
- When possible, force wealthy targets into areas where they are unfamiliar with how to operate the equipment, such as phone booths or dinghies or gas stations.
- Save for last the overeducated sleuths tracking your origins and whereabouts. A doughy dessert is a welcome palate cleanser.

1.3 Immigration law compliance

IF YOU HAVE arrived in the hull of a ship, you will not need a visa to travel to a port of entry. Customs and Border Protection immigration officers will patrol right next to you, pause to scan the area, and yet not see you there on top of a wooden crate. Realistically, there are too many of you coming through the port for anyone to process the paperwork anyway.

Although new employees sometimes submit the Employment Eligibility Verification Form I-9 voluntarily, it is not necessary to do so. The fact that you are "an illegal" from a place that is considered "exotic" will add gravitas to your activities. Your foes may splinter, bickering among themselves about whose "fault" it is that you're here.

1.4 New employee orientation

GAINING ADVANTAGE THROUGH the sheer size of the staff requires each worker at this organization to put forth the absolute strongest effort, while also being mindful of workplace safety. Pay careful attention to procedures covered at orientation sessions, especially those designed to prevent accidents, including inadvertent cannibalism.

The orientation will cover secret codes and signals. It will also include an overview of the company history, an explanation of the company vision, mission, values, goals, and a continental breakfast.

ONBOARDING INTO THE
NEW CULTURE

A TEAM IS only as strong as its weakest members. It's inevitable that some will lack the necessary verve to be part of a dynamic, ambitious organization that traverses the length of the Amazon or flies coast to coast. Such mismatches become apparent when the individuals fall back and drop dead.

A few of the more subtle warning signs that someone is not a team player include inflexibility, attendance problems, taking self-ies, and being unimpressed. Note especially anyone who celebrates *birthdays* in the break room—occasions during which individu-als are lavished with gifts and store-bought cake for the dubious accomplishment of survival.

It should be noted that a truly equitable work environment means forgoing "recognition" and the expectation of divisive, time-consuming rewards and activities linked to it.

1.5 Benefits and services not attached to this position:

- Promotions
- Likes
- Parking spaces
- Badges
- Chocolates
- Regalia
- Patches
- Gift cards
- Awards
- Vests
- Fountain pens
- Bonuses
- Medals
- Trophies
- Gold stars
- Sashes
- Placards
- Applause
- Titles
- Certificates
- Diplomas

1.6 Dress code

COULDN'T BLAZERS OR tiaras be distributed to *everyone*? While this is theoretically feasible, the reality is that both sparkly headwear and "recognition blazers" are impractical for swarming.

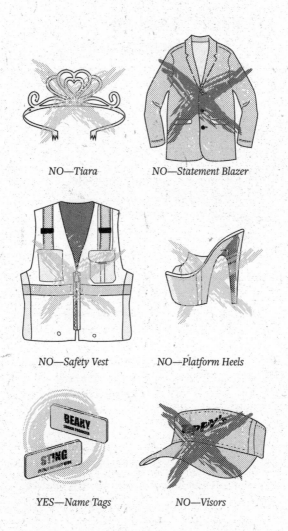

NO—Tiara   NO—Statement Blazer

NO—Safety Vest   NO—Platform Heels

YES—Name Tags   NO—Visors

2 Nondisclosure and Confidentiality

AS A CONDITION of employment, employees must sign a nondisclosure agreement. Employees improperly disclosing trade secrets are subject to disciplinary action, including extermination.

Your organization's success is partially due to some sharp and *pokey* body parts that everyone in the group possesses. It is crucial that no one outside the organization understands in advance just *how* sharp and pokey the group can be.

If you want to be a good team player, do not discuss pending targets and consumption strategies with strangers. Instead, wait until training days to ask important questions, such as:

- How did I get here?
- Why can't I seem to leave?
- What is our budget?
- Do we have a deadline?
- Will we swarm from above or below?
- How many collective loops or swoops do I need to prepare?

- Will we emit sounds?
- As a newcomer, will I be assigned a particular area, like lips?
- Are any other areas my responsibility? Can I say no to crotch?
- What is the "perfect ending" to this project?

In addition to providing clarity about what you're going to do, asking questions at the appropriate time will demonstrate your interest and help you fulfill your role to the best of your abilities.

3 Timekeeping

TIME WORKED IS time actually spent performing assigned duties. Altering, falsifying, tampering with time records, or recording time on another employee's time record could result in disciplinary action, including extermination. However, time records are never reviewed.

3.1 Work hours

THE ORGANIZATION IS always open, and employees must be available on short notice.

3.2 Lunch breaks

LUNCH BREAKS—PERIODS DURING which employees stop lunching (usually because they are *full*)—will occur.

3.3 Other break periods

SOMETIMES, THE ENTIRE organization will disappear and become silent. These break periods are crucial to creating the mistaken assumption that "They're gone."

Be sure to respect these *dormant hours*. It should not be that hard to treat everyone the way you would like to be treated, since everyone is exactly the same as you. For example, if you are a piranha, and thousands of you need to be up early for a full day of racing toward the open seas (as a key stage of the world domination project), then being active at night after quiet hours will make it hard for everyone to rest up enough to eat swimmers from the nearby summer camp along the way. The rules are there to keep the group in balance, and following them can help everything go smoothly.

3.4 Flextime

IF YOU'VE EVER worked with a team, you understand the need to pivot quickly sometimes. Depending on your life cycle, you may find that that the group members have entirely changed by the end of the project. These things happen. Instead of droning on about "the good old days," make yourself useful by mentoring hatchlings.

Being able to remain positive, come what may, in a constantly changing environment is a crucial skill—and your cohorts will likely take notice, unless they don't.

3.5 Emergency closings

INDIVIDUALS MAY DROP out due to issues with abusive substances like flypaper, budgets may be reduced, or the whole group may be doused with gasoline. In emergencies, employees will receive official notification from the company to buzz or scream in a more frenzied manner than usual. It's possible that such events can lead to permanent closure, depending on the extent of the damage. However, usually two or more of you will survive, and it will be strongly implied that you'll procreate and this will all start again.

3.6 Overtime

CONNECTING WITH COLLEAGUES can really enrich your experience. If there are events being held in your shared living space, attend them! If someone suggests having a house potluck night, be the first to sign up to bring a hot dish. A few hot dishes to consider are Joan Van Ark, Suzanne Somers, or William Shatner.

Let's say you are a bird. Are you an early riser? Why not regurgitate some extra worms for the next ones to wake up? If you're going to check out a cool event up the coast in Bodega Bay, ask if anyone wants to tag along.

Overtime will be compensated with intangible dividends only.

Failure to receive proper authorization to work overtime may result in disciplinary action, such as extermination.

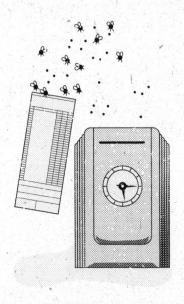

Remember to clock out!

4 Code of Conduct

EMPLOYEES ARE EXPECTED to follow codes, and also to follow whoever's in front of them. Deviations from company rules or the company's flight paths may lead to disciplinary action, such as extermination.

It's true that being thrust into a situation where you need to cohabitate with strangers, who all look and move exactly the way you do, can be difficult and confusing, especially for fledglings and fingerlings who don't have any perceptions of themselves or others—but you stand a much better chance of feeling at home if you yourself are a good colleague and housemate.

Being friendly doesn't mean you need to be friends with everyone—it simply means being someone who's pleasant to be pressed against, someone who can keep your beak or teeth to yourself when not in use. Introduce yourself to anyone whose thorax is touching yours, say hello when you slide over someone, and be cordial with housemates in coworking spaces, such as carcasses.

A "good housemate" doesn't just eat waste and make noise (though these courtesies should not be underestimated). Rather, living with others means eschewing boundaries and personal space.

4.1 Travel policy

YOU MAY NEED to travel for company purposes. This includes trips to:

- The desert
- The Lakewood Manor Hotel
- Towns in Texas
- Swarm conferences, where you'll represent the company
- Eye sockets

For this kind of travel, don't forget to keep track of your per diem expenses.

If you're used to living in a relatively sheltered wood, meadow, or cove with family, or with just a few hundred roommates, the idea of this kind of business travel may be a little scary. However, if you're willing to risk leaving your comfort zone and time zone, there are many perks, such as being able to take down herds of cattle or snorkeling tourists.

4.2 Workplace safety

THE COMPANY GIVES information to employees about health issues and workplace safety through:

- Training sessions
- Meetings
- Ultrasonic messaging
- Memos
- Physical interventions

Disciplinary action, including extermination, may be taken against you if you violate safety standards, create dangerous situations, or fail to remedy such situations.

Avoid antisocial behaviors that could lead to tussles, like coughing up undigested toenails or smiling.

Some ways you can reduce hazards are by discarding old skulls (or putting them in the dishwasher) in a timely manner; knitting old skin and clothing fibers into your nest right away, instead of leaving them sitting around on corpses; and putting any hairballs you make into the trash can.

4.3 Nondiscrimination

YOUR NEW ORGANIZATION does not discriminate on the basis of differences, mainly because there are few. Studying one another is not the goal of the operation, and anyone found doing so may be exterminated.

4.4 Visitors in the workplace

THE COMPANY DOES not allow visitors. Be aware of this policy so you don't make others uncomfortable, especially the guests, who might be eaten. Failure to adhere to this policy may result in extermination.

4.5 Building security

EMPLOYEES ARE RESPONSIBLE for security during any Break Periods/Dormant Hours. They will set alarms and check the perimeter. Employees with work keys are responsible for them.

It may seem like a minor issue, but simple things like discussing who's going to be the last one out of the mound, hive, roost, or underwater cave can make a mass exodus more efficient. Your colleagues want to feel that they're sharing a space with someone who is conscious of safety and comfort each time they all attempt to exit together forcefully through a very small hole. Don't forget to turn off lights and hot plates.

4.6 Staff meetings

STAFF MEETINGS WILL be held *24 hours a day*. These meetings allow employees to be informed about company activities and important news.

To ensure that these meetings run smoothly, you should work to understand what's shared and what's not. Just kidding. Everything is shared. If you want to stay alive, it's best to use resources as they become available. Ignore labels in the pantry or fridge, and assume that all items are for communal use. If you want tempting things, just take them! It is a good idea to do neck exercises in case a *tug-of-war* breaks out between two or more parties.

5 Social Security

THE ILLUSTRIOUS GROUP you have joined has a proven track record of success, predicated on projects with clear goals, which include everything from spinning whole towns in spiderwebs to swooping into hairdos to ruining spring break in the Amazon River.

Human resistance to the group is feeble because humans do not excel at working together (and they even work against one another)—thus they have no social security. Also, humans stand very far apart, as much as several inches. It's easy to cover their entire bodies, all 360 degrees of which are *always* exposed. The only small part that's sometimes unavailable is their feet, often encased in thick *shoes*. This is why you tend to find remains of humans taking the form of feet—hiking boots protruding from webs, Adidas stump bobbing in the lake, etc.

6 Technology Policy

PHONES ARE HORRIBLE inventions that can ruin *everything*. While large groups like yours have historically had great success, the presence of phones, especially in modern times, may reduce the chances of survival by up to 100 percent. The threat they pose is multifaceted:

- Phone orders: Usually, the fires that rain down from the sky are the result of a *favor*, typically an *air strike*, that a guy in khakis *called in* from his old military buddy. Warning signs include human cupping hand over a phone, whispering, and turning away. All of these will be done while giving the *side-eye*.
- Find my friends: You would not be careless enough to lose your friends. But hostile actors could locate you with phones, radar, or satellites. It is best to disable these features, something accomplishable by *swarming* the towers to *jam* them. Success is indicated by a repetitive noise, like "Bob? Bob? Bob?"
- Call and notification sounds: Loud ringers or text message alert sounds can be really distracting, especially if your group makes its own loud ringing sounds and alerts. Adjust your sounds to the highest volume, especially if you're in the coworking space, so everyone can stay focused. Hopefully, you will drown out the humans, evident when they press phones hard to their heads and squint like it hurts.
- Taking calls: If all else fails, head outside to *take* calls. This may involve knocking down humans to dislodge phones from their cheeks or possibly eating their hands. By offering this courtesy to your colleagues, you ensure that there will be no distractions as they complete the project.

7 Procedure for Handling Complaints

EMPLOYEES WHO HAVE job-related questions or complaints should work to resolve them on their own. Being passive-aggressive can really throw off the energy in a co-living and -working space. Plus, no one will notice.

When you're living and working with a group, it's natural for some conflicts to arise. Most of the time, these can be resolved with a squawk or a quick nip.

However, some individuals won't get the hint. Never is this more common than when you are an insect and the organization's structure includes a queen (see below).

7.1 Disciplinary action

THE ORGANIZATION HOLDS each of its members to its rules and standards of conduct. No one should deviate from them, regardless of royal rank. Some actions are grounds for immediate extermination.

There might be somebody who:

- gobbles others' food out of their mouths.
- uses company equipment without authorization.
- never does their dishes.
- is constantly and loudly laying eggs.
- reveals company business practices.

Try to communicate with *whomever* is causing the problem and confront her. If this effort is unsuccessful, it may be appropriate to begin disciplinary proceedings.

7.2 Union policy and performance reviews

IF THERE'S AN ongoing problem, even after you have communicated and tried to talk it out with the queen, it's time to get the union involved. Blind allegiance to a queen will always be an exploitable weak spot for any swarm, flock, school, drove, brood, colony, murder, or horde. If she is poached, manipulated, or headhunted, the whole organization will go down.

Performance reviews are occasions during which employees and queens can talk about ideas for meeting work goals.

❑ **DON'T FEEL AWKWARD ABOUT ROCKING THE HIVE—** Maybe it's something trivial, such as the way she never contributes to making wax or feeding all those larvae, but addressing issues as they occur is more mature than letting them fester. Life is short— about 20 days.

❑ **MAKE CLEAR YOUR VISION—** The queen is the only one with differing views on what constitutes a good time, so it's important to think collectively about whether this individual is contributing to the overall office vibe. As a colleague, she is rude and doesn't want to get to know you. Keep an open mind and recognize that she may have things going on in her life, like mating with drones. Try to be as polite, open, and friendly as you can. But consider extermination. If you do this, you will spontaneously develop your own ovaries anyway. So, it's not as though the group will be short on eggs.

- ❑ **CONTRIBUTE TO THE EFFORT TO TRANSITION AWAY FROM A MONARCHY–** It may be tempting to ignore something that needs to be done, such as changing the toilet roll or overthrowing your queen, and think, "Oh, well. Someone else will do it." However, everyone in the group can and should be regarded as *someone*. There ought never be a need to pledge fealty.

7.3 Extermination

EMPLOYEES SHALL BE given as much as two minutes' notice before extermination. Since employment with the organization is based on mutual consent, both parties have the right to terminate the relationship. However, typically, employees offer the courtesy of dying rather than leaving.

All company property, including lanyards, will be retrieved from exterminated employees.

8 Have FUN!

LAST BUT CERTAINLY not least, have fun! You're likely in this situation for the very practical reason of having a nice place to stay and work, but you're also here to eat new foods and enjoy new sensations. It won't always be as easy, but you might just create some of your best memories, even long-term ones, if your brain has the capacity to do that. Enjoy!

SHELTERING AND AGING IN PLACE:

Tech Made Easy for Vampires

SO, YOU'VE HIT the big 6-0-0. You might be thinking—*So what?* After all, you've had 599 previous birthdays. Probably. Who keeps track? *Bah!*

You've undoubtedly noticed that the modern age has brought substantial changes. A few are welcome, notably the broader selection of caskets, which now offer enticing options, such as Bluetooth and tanning beds.

However, most of the societal changes are repugnant, including the rise of *jeans*, which you would never wear but do have to look at. They appear to be very stiff trousers that manage to be at once unattractive, constricting in the *master john goodfellow* area, and difficult to puncture. What's worse, if 600 years has taught you anything, it's that if jeans (or other dandy hallmarks of modern times) were simply going to vanish, they would have done so by now, like the quill pen or common courtesy.

Let's be clear. Age isn't just a number. Such a long life of solitude and success has made you too trusting for the world in which you find yourself. You may have pioneered early phishing schemes and identity theft, but you now find yourself vulnerable to them.

Still, why bother with becoming a late adapter? To be blunt, humans require only a little sensitive information to destroy everything you've built. If they obtain your identity and location, you will be subject to sunlight, wooden stakes, crossbows, holy water, crucifixes, wolfsbane, decapitation, fire, shovel attacks, and stale communion wafers. The Jitterbug phone stashed in your coffin glove box for emergencies is not going to save you. The battery isn't even charged.

If you're not using a computer, the changes in the modern world are more extensive than you may realize. Societal attitudes have changed toward the aristocracy, toward the seduction of teen girls by ancient men, and so much more:

- While your peerage rank of count sits above viscount and baron, this is not what's meant anymore by "status."
- Rulers now emerge via popularity competitions in which only half of commoners "vote," which means that the ruler isn't even popular. But the ruler is still not you.
- Unusual goings-on cannot be connected legally to "witchcraft" and pinned on mortals.
- People keep many animals within their domiciles now, including pigs and ferrets, and yet are prone to enlist wildlife removal services for bats, such as yourself.
- Few teens have *convivial society anymore*, not even with each other. They certainly do not wish to do so with you.
- There's an obsession with the future, with predictions for everything—the weather, the population, the economy, Fantasy Football. No one wants surprises, especially the kind you provide.
- It's challenging to create new vampires for a coven because people keep embalming them, cremating them, or ejecting them into space in eco-pods.
- No matter how fast you move, security cameras catch your cape.

The modern age is all about communication, which is hard for introverts. But with a change to a 21st-century mind-set—essential for anyone over 500 who wants success, romance, and a pristine torso—you have the power to make connections that turn into something more nutritious. Those zeroes don't have to resemble the fatal stab holes that overconfidence in your relevance will create.

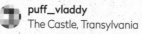

puff_vladdy
The Castle, Transylvania

239 likes
puff_vladdy #mirrorselfie #ootd #thedrip

A GUIDE TO THE COMPUTER

EVERYBODY IS INTO it—and that includes seniors. In fact, a growing number of vampires over 500 are learning to use the power button and to "save" things, giving them better access to communication and reducing the frequency of comments, such as "Where'd it go? I hate this thing."

The first thing you need to do is demand that Renfield get you a computer and/or mobile device, as these items link to others when connected to the *internet*, a worldwide telecommunications system. Wail like a banshee when he tells you how much it cost.

A newbie needs to know a few things to get started, such as how to create strong passwords like 1234 and 6666, and, most importantly, to divine information about everyone else while remaining mum about your own. This is called "lurking," a skill you already possess.

To enjoy the perks of the internet while avoiding potential perils, review this quick "cheat sheet" of terms you might encounter. Keep in mind that there are no physical *sheets* anymore, whether for cheating or other purposes. Almost all words these days related to objects or actions are figurative and should be represented with "quotation marks."

Icons

YOU ARE AN icon. The items in question are "icons." Instead of an actual object that you can touch, like a folder, paper, or an abacus, you will maneuver an "arrow" and "click" it on an image of that thing. This click action might (but probably won't) create a sound that you'd consider a click, and this sound will have no relationship to the sounds an actual arrow would make.

In any case, this movement opens a "program," where you'll be able to engage in "activities" that barely have any association with items for which they are named. Case in point, an "active" user involved in "activities" is typically in a state that resembles catatonia.

It should be noted that these "icons" will be very small, in spite of the massive size the word suggests. They won't be labeled and will be in different locations on every device, clumped together in weird configurations like tiny herds of deer.

Mouse

THIS ITEM IS the clicker mentioned above. If *The Flintstones* were still on TV, this would be an actual mouse, but it isn't. Originally, this gadget looked like an elephant tampon. There aren't many elephants in the Carpathian Mountains of Transylvania, and tampons weren't invented until 1929, so this may or may not be a helpful reference point. In any case, these days, the "mouse" is a touch pad. The corresponding arrow on the screen is much smaller than the fingertip used to operate it. Again, this can be challenging for someone with the vision of a bat. The mouse also proves a struggle for people who suffer from arthritis, a lack of body heat, or a condition called *undead fingernails*.

Caps lock

WHEN YOU PRESS this button once, all the letters you type will be capitalized. Use this whenever you want to. Press it again when you want to. Don't overthink it.

Delete key

THE DELETE KEY will erase words to the left of the cursor. The words to the right of the cursor remain for all eternity, especially if the mouse is inoperable.

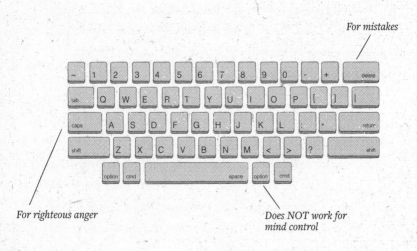

For mistakes

For righteous anger

Does NOT work for mind control

The Keyboard

Scroll

YOU ARE UNDOUBTEDLY one of the few individuals around here with experience of actual scrolls made of parchment or even vellum on fancy occasions. As the count of your county, you probably have composed a decree or two. Use the "scroll" feature to "unfurl" the "pages" of "documents" or "sites."

Doomscroll

TAKE NOTE THAT some pages do not end. They "unfurl" forever, as if one rides an elevator to Middle Earth, and the screen is a window tracking one's progress to hell. These are often called "feeds" because looking at them can be comparable to a binge-eating experience that leaves one with despair and the urge to lie around in roomy clothing.

Predictive text

WHEN YOU TYPE into the search "bar" on a search "engine," the computer will try to guess what you're going to type, though it will always be wrong. For example, if you want to locate *virgin blood*, the computer will offer to fetch *virgin coconut oil*.

Attachments

DESPITE HOW IT sounds, "attachments" have nothing to do with emotional connections, though it's possible to become emotional in response to them. To "open" something is to "click" on it. People called *hackers* or *scammers* will "mail" you "documents" or "pages" in hopes that you'll open them. If you do, something terrible will happen. You might think you can save yourself by turning into a bat or a wolf or whatever, but it won't help because the target of the attack isn't you. It's your "identity." Previously, your identity was mainly your name and the rumors people told about you at the tavern. It might not seem so bad to have someone assume the burden of your identity for a while. However, a lot of "money" is at stake, something about which you must be particularly vigilant because money is invisible now, shrunk to fit inside "chips" and "apps," neither of which are food.

Turning your computer on and off

NO ONE REALLY knows how to do this. Just close it. Complain when it doesn't work until someone says, "Did you reboot it?" And then say, "Shut up," and go into another room and try to locate a button somewhere. Mutter to yourself about the *fiddly-dad* until you find it. Promptly forget where it was.

The On/Off Button

REDUCED MOBILITY IN the daytime makes life isolating, which may tempt you to leave the lair. However, outside the lair is where the problems are—the stakings and beheadings. One great thing about the modern age is that you can now make the most of your tedious daytime hours. You used to stare at the coffin lining for 14 hours, just daydreaming about Lucy or Mina or whatever. Depression, boredom, and loneliness have long been endemic to retirement, even temporary retirement. But with the technology today, vampires may be able to avoid all that negative stuff and live their best afterlives ever!

Selecting HIBERNATE or SLEEP on the computer provides a power-saving mode that makes your "documents" and "programs" available in an instant when you start again. They're not gone forever like the covens of vampire brides that Jonathan Harker likes to kill when he visits. That guy is quite impatient toward people with hairy palms and God forbid anyone sleeps with their eyes open. At any rate, when you retire to your quarters each day, you can pick up where you left off, shopping for blood banks or frilly shirts. Convenient when the sun rises quickly at the equinoxes or when that other jerk, Van Helsing, shows up. You're a vibrant, vital individual, and it's crucial for you to remain engaged, whether that means watching the bat-cam at the zoo or other forms of erotic content. Hibernation is for machines now, not for you.

Wallpaper

THIS IS AN image that you can put on the "wall" of your computer. It can be anything you enjoy viewing, really, but one suggestion is to post a *selfie*. Since you don't have a reflection, it has been a while since you devoted proper attention to your appearance. By studying your features all the time, you can obsess over your flaws. You can generate a list of *procedures* you would like to have performed on your face. Computer cameras exaggerate the size of your nose, for example. You may wish to have Renfield bring in a doctor who can shrink your nose to a size that will make your 'nose' look better.

Don't be afraid to personalize!

Changing Your Wallpaper

Making the most of it

SO, LET'S SAY you've joined the growing group of vampires learning how to use technology and social media. Not only do you have your own email account, but now you're actively doing Google searches, as well as browsing Facebook and Twitter newsfeeds and watching YouTube. Obviously, you've discovered that there's so much more you can do with what's in front of you—read large-print e-books, play solitaire, post videos that propagate conspiracy theories, and share pictures of people without their permission. You can even watch the latest TV shows, like *Bonanza* or *The Honeymooners*. Why stop there? There's so much more that is at your exceptionally long fingertips! The internet isn't as safe as an actual dark alley. On the other hand, it can provide an extremely comfortable life. While away your daytime hours with "high-fiving" unremarkable activities, such as eating snacks or having feelings or remaining anonymous to torch-wielding villagers.

E-pistles

NO ONE WRITES with pen and paper anymore. One benefit is that without a postmark or a return address, it is unlikely that Johnny Harker comes to your place anymore posing as a librarian or a real estate agent or whatever it is this time. But if he does dox you somehow, he's going to sit in his room and post his every thought and intention via Instagram. It's a modern version of the same bright-boy move he always made in the past—jotting down in letters and diary entries his true identity as a vampire hunter, as well as all of his intricate plans. You don't have to follow him anymore. All you need to do is "follow" him.

AS YOU'VE DISCOVERED, there are "social" "sites" that you can "visit." As overwhelming as these sites can be, they have the potential to foster connections in unprecedented ways. No longer must you spend long hours on your feet at balls, wearing confining fancy clothes and elaborate brooches, waltzing the night away in order to dazzle potential conquests. It can all be done while you lie on your back in a comfy tracksuit. You can be "social" now instead of social, perusing these living à la carte menus during the daytime in a darkened room or in bed. Don't be afraid to look up people you've never tasted before. You'll quickly learn if your new "friends" are married, if they have children, and what sort of diet they're fattening themselves up with. You'll even have the chance to weigh in on where they go on vacation. Use LinkedIn to drop a casual "Hi" to interesting men you've met at events. You will find out exactly where they work! Actually, women are allowed to leave the house unaccompanied now, so you might meet some of them, as well.

By far, the ultimate places to peruse snacks are dating sites. No matter your palate, these sites are menus for easy smorgasbords.

- For a huge inventory, check out Match. The food may be bland, but there's certainly a lot of it.
- For anyone who finds romance exhausting, try Tinder. The humans who use it are in search of *hookups*, which is exactly what it sounds like—you'll be invited to hook something of yours into something of theirs.
- For the clean eater, eHarmony forces members to fill out endless questionnaires. You can probably find out your potential paramours' blood types here. You can also find out who's certified vegan (i.e., *grass-fed*), organic, and/or living a free-range, cubicle-free existence.
- For someone who likes to keep it classic, there's a site called *ChristianCafe*. This is truly comfort food from the Old Country.

NEW FREEDOMS

IT'S EASIER THAN ever to rent an AirBnB in a country that has long nights—you can even enjoy darkness 24/7. For example, consider wintering in Finland for half the year and Patagonia for the other half. You'll barely need to be isolated ever again, and the fact that your skin is always cold won't seem notable! The trickiest part will be the journey itself, but you've already proven many times over that you know how to stow away in the hull of a ship and subsist on crew members.

As another option, instead of going on tour, consider a residency in Las Vegas. Casinos have no daylight, ever, and it's a snap to blend in. Nearly everyone possesses an undead pallor. Capes are a dime a dozen, though you may wish to consider bejeweling yours to assimilate better with the locals. The blood-alcohol levels will give you a heady rush in Vegas, but beware of so-called "drunk texting," which is communicating online while under the influence of blood-alcohol. You may communicate things that you didn't intend. A seemingly innocent exchange that you initiate with *Where you at, gurl?* could lead to someone finding out where *you're* at. The potential for missteps is compounded in public forums such as Facebook or Twitter, where private data can be used against you. Temper online messages by asking yourself if you'd be comfortable with Van Helsing seeing them.

TROLLING

TROLLING ISN'T JUST for trolls anymore. Online darkness provides superior hunting ground to darkness IRL. Create multiple accounts so that you can hunt as a pack all by yourself, posing not only as a straightforward hater, but also as a link-spammer; a reassurance junkie; a brony, overused memes guy; and other types that make humans sad. Sad humans who have been trolled in any of these ways are statistically more likely to accept an invitation from a friend to come over for Mountain Dew and Slim Jims. Sit back and wait to become that friend. For online humans with no likes on their profiles, an hour is a really long time.

/r/lonelysadhumans:

[-] jealousgurrl · 1 day ago
I am "obsessed" with "stalking" my ex-boyfriend's new girlfriend on social media. I don't know how to stop! I could just die!
permalink save report reply

> **[-] freakinglovecats** ⇝ jealousgurrl · 7 hours ago
> You could go for a walk or start a community garden. Get a volunteer job. See a therapist, for sure.
> permalink save report reply

> **[-] JohnnyNoMates** ⇝ jealousgurrl · 5 hours ago
> I used to be obsessed with my ex, too, and now she has a restraining order. Definitely don't go down that rabbit hole.
> permalink save report reply

> > **[-] Vlad69** ⇝ jealousgurrl · 2 minutes ago ✪
> > Definitely go down my hole.
> > permalink save report reply

BEING AN ONLINE influencer will reduce anyone's desire to be in your physical presence by 63 percent. Gone will be the days of being harassed in your own home by a pesky Van Helsing or Johnny Harker type. As another perk, the ad revenue will reduce by 100 percent the number of workplace webinars you are required to attend (e.g., *"We Need to Talk": Difficult Conversations at Work*).

Creating polls is an easy and fun way to establish camaraderie with like-minded individuals. Although you're alone in your casket, the magic of the internet brings other vampires out of the "woodwork." Suddenly, you've got people to talk to besides the ones you'll eat. And you didn't even have to create them!

 Vlad created a poll
Oct 24 at 8:12pm

Your answers are in! And the suspicions were correct. If you're like Prince and rarely leave home, people will regard your velvet waistcoat as intriguing, not creepy. Here's our next poll:

☐	I was attacked at least once in the 20th century with a sharpened broomstick because I ate an employee at a mall.		+87
☐	I have not been attacked with a sharpened broomstick since the advent of Amazon Prime.		+70
☑	I last left the house before 2005.		+90
☐	The last time I spoke on the phone in my mysterious accent was before 2010.		+83

OTHER WAYS TO MAKE THE MOST OF DORMANT HOURS

FOR "BUILDING" WEALTH:

- Watch videos on how to make money on *E-Trade*. Eternity is the perfect amount of time to invest in exchange-traded funds.
- Create a closed FB group for your friends called Nocturnal Daytraders.
- Start a YouTube wealth management channel, *Rich Vlad/Poor Vlad*.
- Establish a deregulation super PAC called *Prosperous Americans for Prosperous Prosperity*.
- Alternatively, sell your services as a hit man on the dark web in exchange for cryptocurrency.

FOR "HUNTING" FOOD:

- Order from Uber Eats to receive a delicious driver right to your door. (Order crawdads or fried crickets for Renfield.)
- Purchase items from Amazon to receive a delicious driver right to your door.
- Sign up for catalogs to receive a delicious mail carrier right to your door.
- Join Craigslist to receive a delicious "massage therapist" right to your door.
- Hack Niantic to designate your lair a Pokémon gym, receiving delicious gamers right to your door.

FOR LEARNING:

- Because the population is older now than ever in the past, look up medical conditions to which you are likely to be exposed when you imbibe seniors, including diabetes and cancer. Will you get these conditions? Dear god, do you have them now?? Check out WebMD.
- If both you and your prey have cataracts, will anyone know what's going on?
- What happens if you ingest Botox or collagen fillers?

HERE ARE A FEW INTERESTING FACTS AND FIGURES:

- 11 percent of Facebook users are vampires.
- 13 percent of vampires 500 years and older are using Twitter.
- There is 1,920 percent yearly growth in this demographic group.
- Four out of five of these users log on for at least 17 hours in any given day.

VAMPIRES USING FACEBOOK:

- 40 percent: Locate "meals"
- 30 percent: Connect with extremely old friends
- 20 percent: Post embarrassing pics of Renfield
- 10 percent: Play Scrabble

CONCLUSION

ALTHOUGH YOU WERE vulnerable in the past each time you went out to eat, there is now no need ever to imperil yourself again. This is truly the era of the vampire! Congratulations.

"Hey, Besties!"

APPENDIX I

A Compendium of Human Repellants

Practically Identical

FANGS

Humans have big, flat front teeth, like horses. They're suitable for eating chard or Craisins. But in a fight? A light switch coverplate would make a better weapon. If you are packing impressive ivory—and, let's face it, anything will be impressive relative to humans, with their amphitheater of molars—flash your wares.

Your Teeth

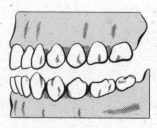

Their Teeth

GLISTENING SALIVA

This makes an especially nice companion to *Fangs*. Produce as much saliva as you can. Eat Sour Patch Kids, an ant colony, etc. Fangs covered in shiny or stringy saliva will ward off humans more effectively than dry ones.

 TIP: Position yourself under moonlight or streetlight, and experiment with different head angles.

STARING

No matter how many times the human says, "Um, can I help you?" you must stare *without speaking*. A steady, unwavering gaze is what wards them off.

Humans actually love to stare at each other until their eyes bulge and they lose mouth control. This typically has the effect of soliciting more engagement, not less. If one catches another in the act, a call-and-response ritual ensues, and this is what must be avoided at all costs. It looks like this:

```
"What are you looking at?" says Human #1, a question
that can be expressed either verbally or nonverbally
via a scowl.

"Nothing," says Human #2. The nonverbal version
involves breaking the stare and pretending that he or
she was about to engage in a casual self-armpit-sniff
anyway. Regardless of how it's conveyed, this response
is a lie.
```

Actually, *Human #2* was admiring that toupee. It matched *Human #1*'s head so perfectly. Where would a person get something like that? Was that real hair? Was there a warranty? Would it be okay to compliment it if the phrasing was just right?

And actually, *Human #1* does want to be looked at. This bus route goes to the audition for a TV program called "Hair Jockeys."

GUTTURAL NOISES

If you are capable of growls or agonized moans, now is the time to release them. Start quiet and get louder. These emissions are another thing that humans want to do quite badly—especially on overbooked flights. The fact that you are doing something they can't will make them retreat and possibly sulk.

HALITOSIS:

Humans eradicate their own bacterial fragrances with blue solvents and pastes, probably to call less attention to those ineffectual teeth. Smelly breath can really set off your fangs, especially if you expend it in a visible cloud. Alternatively, "death breath" can be a special calling card for hordes: *Hello there, I'm decaying.*

*A Human Foolishly
Dispelling His Halitosis*

CASH

Money can both attract and repel humans, mainly because of cryptocurrency. But cash has universal appeal. The well-placed bundle of bank notes can dampen any desire to protect humanity, or even just the guy with the pet ferrets. Use with caution—they'll go where the loot is, and if you keep it too close, you may wake up to hands groping your mourning suit, thorax, sack dress, or motherboard.

REDUCED VISIBILITY

Humans imagine that if they can see you, they can take you down. Thus, you won't eat them or conquer them. Put them off their game by carrying out your activities in these environments:

- Fog
- Trees
- Corn maze
- Romantic restaurant
- Blizzard
- Tomb
- Basement/stoner's bedroom
- Mist
- Murk

- Ocean
- Smoggy futuristic city
- Wormhole
- Rustic cabin
- Moors
- Ghost ship
- Anyplace that has "passageways" (Castle, Space station, etc)
- The IKEA marketplace

TIP: Don't forget about speed. Let them glimpse just a tail, a fin, a glowing eye, an undead sidekick. If the surprise has its effect, the humans will exclaim *Wassat?*, followed by *Shhhh* and *Stop shushing me*.

DEAD ZONE (TYPE 1)

Consider filling your lair, tomb, ship, or hive with dead human bodies. They don't like those.

DEAD ZONE (TYPE 2)

Spend your time in an area with no cell phone signal.

Use a fog machine so you don't have to rely on mother nature!

EGO STROKING

Humans like to feel that they've been brave, that they're not cowards. Sometimes when they have the sense that they've been victorious, they'll go away to tell their friends. If you're able to speak, here are some phrases to practice:

"I'll be feeling *that* in the morning."

"How is it that you always look great, even in sweatpants?"

"Have you considered becoming an executioner—like, professionally?"

"Every time you're knocked down, you get back up. You're the most perfect you there is."

"That's a sick rocket launcher. I believe a large sexual member correlates to such a device."

"You are even more beautiful on the inside than on the outside!" (For the one who keeps fighting, even with entrails spilling)

INSECTS

This is, of course, excellent news for many types of swarms. Your very existence is a human repellant. For everyone else, consider recruiting insects to your headquarters. Cockroaches, for example, have mastered audible footfalls—the telltale "skittle" across linoleum or metallic potato chip bags. (See "Reduced visibility.")

> **TIP:** Spiders are not technically insects, but since 3.5 percent of humans have arachnophobia, they are an excellent choice, as well (the closer to human-hand—sized, the better). Spiders are maestros of the "slow walk," normally toward a face or a crotch.

PUBLIC SPEAKING

Since 25 percent of the human population fears this more than death or even being asked to dance, why not set up a PowerPoint presentation in your hideout, and perhaps a cardboard audience taped to ballroom chairs from the Holiday Inn? When the human bursts into the place, fingers looped in some grenades, say, "Where have you been? Everyone's waiting." Turn on the projector.

> **TIP:** Keep an IT ghoul on retainer to wrangle the clicker, locate a Mac-compatible cord, troubleshoot the Wi-Fi, etc.

MUCUS

Can you secrete, exude, or spew? Maybe your mucus provides a protective coating from the toxic, bio-luminescent substance in the cavern where you live or maybe you're just phlegmy from all those guttural noises. Either way, embrace the green stuff. The presence of mucus has been proven to increase your odds of survival in your first skirmish with humans by 11 percent.

> **TIP:** Slithering makes an excellent companion to mucus. It requires some flexibility through the hips. Practice in a mirror if you are visible there.

INTIMACY

The only thing humans dislike more than solitude is commitment. Here are some useful phrases that may repel humans:

```
"Where do you see this relationship going?"
"Would you like to meet my sire/offspring/egg sac/
colony?"
"Let's take a trip together."
"Did you get my text?"
```

HEIGHTS

You may be tempted to hide in a burrow or cave. But consider looking up! Humans are afraid of heights, and they should be. They do not have claws, wings, or upper-body strength, nor do they have any landing capabilities. In fact, they fall end over end like bowling pins, and they bounce on contact. This is one of their more logical fears. If you choose a mountaintop lair, they will have to hike there, which will offer plenty of time for them to argue about who was supposed to pack the Clif bars. It will also allow you time to prepare the PowerPoint presentation (see "Public speaking").

 CAUTION: If you have no wings or landing capabilities yourself, there is some folly in choosing this option.

OVERSHARE

No human wants an honest account of you. Discuss any of the following topics, and even the most aggressive human is likely to vacate the premises:

- poor self-worth
- hating one's mother
- lesions or discharges
- paucity of followers on one's IG
- overheated circuitry
- loving or hating Hallmark movies
- "All these maggots are itchy"

CAUTION: While most humans will be put off by over-sharing, the ones who are not may be of special concern. Watch for one-upmanship (i.e., human hates self/mother more than you, has runnier lesions, saw a maggot once, etc.). Worse than a human who wants to bludgeon you is one who "feels you." You will think, *Why don't I just rip this person's jawbone off the hinge?* But it will somehow seem complicated.

PUBLIC DISPLAYS OF AFFECTION

Mating behavior, especially in a Starbucks, tends to be repugnant to humans. They bring their hands to their eyes, leading some experts to believe that they experience a burning sensation. The more tongue that's involved, the more acute the discomfort seems to be. If a gang of aggressive humans approaches, you may be tempted to eat a few—that's probably your idea of engaging your tongue. But, for now, grab one of your minions and make out with it instead.

TIP: When humans witness mating displays on their computer screens rather than at the mall, especially screens within their dwellings or cubicles, the opposite effect can occur—a kind of hypnosis. Reduce the number of humans who'll notice your hunting or colonizing activities by loading their devices with titles like *Pulp Friction* or *Shaving Ryan's Privates*. Even if they don't exactly like the films, they'll be curious about how the friction and shaving will play out.

Humans love the notion of individuality. *In 200,000 years of humanity, no one has ever been quite like me.* But all of those unique "me's" tend to choose the same passwords—*123456, password, letmein,* and their ilk. Any type of identity theft challenges their collective view of themselves as irreplaceable. But if the notion of an imposter charging a Paula Deen Coastal Breeze Eurotop mattress is destabilizing, imagine the reaction when you show up wearing the human's own face! Bonus: What are they going to do? Attack themselves?

More Human Repellants to Consider

- ☐ Exposed intestines
- ☐ Group text messages
- ☐ Furniture assembly
- ☐ Noise of bones crushing, especially done slowly
- ☐ Cottage cheese
- ☐ AutoCorrect
- ☐ Preorbital gland marking
- ☐ Putting bags on the seat next to you
- ☐ The word *moist*
- ☐ Clowns
- ☐ Vomiting acid
- ☐ Inauthenticity
- ☐ Discussion of CBD supplements
- ☐ Social licking/nibbling
- ☐ Blocking sidewalk for selfie or belfie
- ☐ Anything impending (change, doom, etc.)
- ☐ Taking up two parking spaces
- ☐ Free tax workshop
- ☐ Threat of lawsuit for staking/beheading
- ☐ Stevia
- ☐ Adding them to a mass email list
- ☐ Consumption of live animals
- ☐ Effusive compliments
- ☐ Brushing teeth in public restroom
- ☐ Long Wi-Fi passwords
- ☐ Kissing when you first meet
- ☐ Small blobs of brain matter
- ☐ Mouth sounds while chewing
- ☐ Paperwork
- ☐ Not wiping down machines you've used at the gym
- ☐ Anything dangling (eyeballs, arms, teeth, air freshener)
- ☐ Silence
- ☐ Confusion over whether to hug or shake hands
- ☐ Work retreat
- ☐ Long coffee order that includes the term "half-caf"
- ☐ Most types of wailing
- ☐ Vague status updates
- ☐ The success of your start-up (see "Ego stroking")

APPENDIX II

A Field Guide
to Humans

LOOK OUTSIDE YOUR lair. What's out there? If you take a moment, you'll notice humans everywhere! There are the usual places, of course—ShopRite and the interstate. If you observe carefully, you might glimpse one in the great outdoors, taking selfies or littering.

Given that humans are so numerous, it can be a challenge to distinguish one from another. Yet, determining which are aggressive, friendly, or nutritious can be crucial to dominating or ignoring them.

Since the middle of the 20th century, the taxonomy of *Homo sapiens* has been subdivided into more subspecies than had previously been identified. The sudden proliferation of new cuts of jeans heightened observers' awareness of variations previously obscured by standard-issue *overcoats*.

If you want to understand humans better, create a habitat in your yard. This need not be expensive or complicated. All it requires is a drive-thru window out of which you will wave small white paper bags. With this small effort, you'll be able to attract cars full of humans, observing vehicular habits, such as stockpiling coins in the cup/lint holder, and you will even witness family dynamics, including squabbles over the radio station, especially in autumn, when it's too early to play Christmas music.

Tips to Identify Human Subspecies

THERE ARE *FIELD* *marks* that provide clues to the identification of human subspecies. Some field marks can be obvious, such as the ornate plumage of *uniforms* related to the medical field, package delivery, or the Rockettes. Other indicators are more subtle, such as the degree of baldness on the American or European Bald Man. Remember that the most important way to identify a human is to look at the actual human.

OTHER MARKINGS

- **RUMP PATCH:** Pay attention to any denim pocket embroidery.
- **CRESTED HANDBAG:** Take note of monograms or whether the person stood in line to buy it.

- **EYE RINGS:** That is, glasses, false eyelashes, dark circles, goggles, etc.

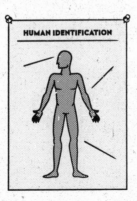

BEHAVIORAL TRAITS ARE important clues to identifying the subspecies of this particular primate. Is this human shy, hiding in some bushes or under a Buick? Or is it charging at you, waving a couple of flares? When you remark on its size and shape, does it get mad?

Some other behavioral questions to consider:

- What's it doing? And should it really be doing that?
- How does it walk? Does it take shortcuts or go the long way?
- How does it fly? First class or coach?
- Does it swim? Or does it wade in the shallows, complaining?
- Does it climb trees? Why?

SONG

A HUMAN'S THEME song can reveal a great deal beyond its obvious presence. Is its theme music moody and instrumental? Or is it Van Halen?

FLOCKING

SOLITARY HUMANS OR family groups are relatively harmless, rarely straying from their roles as runners and screamers. However, when adult humans form into nonfamilial gangs, one must be on alert. An ensemble of four to six adults will feature a male leader and no more than one female. Among the subordinate males, common subspecies might include *Bandanna-headed Sidekick* and *Hairy Nervous Chatterbox*. These men tell a lot of jokes. But don't be fooled. Collectively, this group can be aggressive. Plus, they can prepare for a fight very quickly because of their reliance on montages.

SOON-TO-BE-MATING PAIRS

THE MALE LEADER and the one female should be considered soon-to-be-mating pairs. It's possible they will mate really, really soon. However, it's more likely that this will happen only relatively soon and you won't actually see it. While soon-to-be-mating pairs are not always aggressive, there are circumstances in which they are likely to be. For example, if the pair locks itself into a walk-in freezer, DO NOT WAIT OUTSIDE THE DOOR, no matter how good it smells in there. Items lying around in freezers nearly always include blunt instruments and raw materials for explosives, as well as alluring dead things that may cause you to lose your train of thought. "Two for one" is great in theory, but there are so many other people to pursue. Don't get fixated.

A Note about Females

WHILE FEMALES ARE generally less aggressive than males, it should be noted that they can almost never be killed, at least in feature films. Experts believe they can only be killed by human male adversaries, and usually in the past, in which case they will still be around as motivational flashbacks.

A Brief Guide to Common Backyard North American Humans

AMERICAN OR EUROPEAN BALD MAN

(also called *Shiny-Capped Badass* or
Shine-Pate Ass Capper)

The temperament of the *American or European Bald Man* is a gruff, muscular energy that conjures bar fights and the leather gloves race-car drivers wear. He will be at least six feet tall and/or will strive to create the illusion of being tall with a "puffed up" gait. He will be entirely bald or have a sandpapery shadow. The noise he makes sounds like *Oi! Oi!* He may also have a catchphrase, something like, *Have a bite of THIS!* If there is perceptible hair around the edges of his head, one should conclude that the individual is, in fact, one of two rarely seen subspecies, a *Shaggy-Ringed Trappist Monk* or a *Combover Dad.* The Bald Man is distinctive in temperament—boisterous, easily provoked, and dogged in his pursuits, which often involve explosives and loud, yellow cars.

Shaggy-Ringed Trappist Monk and *Combover Dad* are not spotted frequently enough to be considered *Common Backyard North American Humans*. However, if one does see them, they are very safe to approach. Their call sounds like, *Hello, Big Fella!* Both are sweet and tender.

ARMOR-BREASTED GLARUS

Identifiable by her push-up armor and her glare, this woman is extremely aggressive. Take the time to listen. There's a telltale swoosh as she slices the air with a large sword that requires a two-handed grip. There's also a grunting battle cry that starts quietly and grows louder as she charges, *aaaaAAAHHH*. She emits noise nearly constantly, and thus is not hard to avoid. Sometimes, but not always, there will be the clink of a gladiator skirt or metal jeggings.

BARE-BELLIED MIDRIFF

This woman's shirt caught on a nail or she ripped it to form a tourniquet. Despite having her tummy exposed directly to the elements, she is unstoppable. Experts have noticed that most female humans in the 21st century have been born with advanced martial arts capabilities, and she is no exception. The sounds she makes are *HAH! HAH!* She can be found flying toward whatever threatens her, feetfirst in high-heeled boots. This woman is not friendly.

HOODED CODER

This human is generally introverted and rarely shows its face. However, one might catch a glimpse in the blue reflection of the device into which it can be found staring. The easiest way to identify the Coder is through the loud tapping of its fingers. Its call sounds like a long sigh. Females of this subspecies are, of course, highly skilled at martial arts, so it is best not to startle them unless you are very big, in which case it doesn't matter. The Coder is neither inherently aggressive, nor inherently friendly, and will basically keep to itself if there's an adequate coffee supply.

BLACK-WHISKERED PERIMETER TRACER

This harmless man can be found walking fence lines. He does not speak at all, and his life span is very short, despite his vigilance and his access to powerful weaponry. He has a sensitive startle reflex that causes him to lurch backward and shoot into the air before he dies for almost no reason. He will make his call before he dies. It sounds like, *Hey! You can't come in here!* These men proliferate easily and thus are in no danger of going extinct. They have a peppery flavor.

BROAD-SHOULDERED GENERAL

The characteristic flat-top head and the gold-adorned uniform make the Broad-shouldered General easy to spot. This man can be found walking briskly. Other, younger men jog alongside him to keep up, taking notes (*Enlisted Chirpy Joes*). His call sounds like, *Get the President on the line!* The General may be friendly or he may be hostile. But in either case, even though he has the entire military at his disposal, he will somehow not have the power to help you or hurt you.

AMERICAN GARDEN HUMANS

─ IDENTIFICATION GUIDE ─

*Female Bare-Bellied
Midriff*

*Male Broad-Shouldered
General*

*Male Hooded
Coder*

BROODING NIGHTHAWK

(common names include *King Grouse*
and *Mourning Dude*)

On first glance, one will spy the Brooding Nighthawk taking whisky shots, typically alone and at night. His backstory is defined by a slain wife, a slain war buddy, or a slain police partner. Other notable features include a diet composed of one old carton of lo mein noodles, short but lustrous hair, and no one who understands his pain. His call sounds like *Sorry, pal. I don't do that anymore.* Regardless of what you do to defend yourself against his very aggressive behavior, the worst injury you can inflict is a nasty-looking gash to the side torso that will slow him down for two to ten minutes—probably because he has been drunk the whole time. It is better to eat him right away, if you hold your liquor well.

COMMON CACKLING PATCH EYE

Men with eye patches are extremely friendly, and it's possible to develop something of a relationship with them. They will release you from any enclosures the Bald Man has put you in. The Patch Eye is named for his distinctive call, *Muahahahahahaha!* It resembles laughter, but, in reality, he is nervous. Judging by the lost eye and the scars, this man has been bullied. He is a terrible fighter, and he badly needs help—often with a very creative entrepreneurial scheme—but he will stand too close to a cliff. He may also fall off some scaffolding or into lava.

COOING HAND EXTENDER

This woman is identifiable by noises like *Shhhh. It's okay. I'm not going to hurt you.* You might be tempted to let her touch your forehead. Take note that the American or European Bald Man follows her everywhere she goes. Stay alert. Do not lean toward her very, very soft-looking fingers.

GOLDEN CHILD CATCHER

This woman assumes the parental role for an orphaned child. The child could be temporarily orphaned or simply could be standing a little too far from its actual parents in the checkout line. In any case, the child is hers now, and she will protect it with a wild abandon that musses her hair and clothing. She often has a blond crest, but may feature other markings. She is identifiable by the way she waves her arms wildly, and makes a call that sounds like, *Take me instead!* The child will be tossed to the side whenever the woman senses danger. It is best to avoid her because the child is an unsafe projectile.

LESSER GARBLED BROAD

(commonly called the *Screech-Damsel*)

This lady makes a few clear calls that sound like *Don't Leave Me!* and *Oh Don!* Experts believe that her mouth doesn't close—as evidenced by near-constant screaming, laughing, or open-mouthed shock. When in peril, she freezes or plays dead, sometimes achieving actual lack of consciousness. She can be found gripping the *Plain White-Collared Know-It-All*'s elbow (see his entry below). The population of Lesser Garbled Broads exploded in the middle of the 20th century, but has since dwindled as *Bare-Bellied Midriffs* usurped their territory.

PECTORAL SURF TEEN

With a mop of blond hair, this unemployed juvenile male is chiefly noted for not being taken seriously. He will try to alert the local sheriff, who will put him in jail instead of investigating whatever it is you are doing to the kids at the movie theater. His call sounds like, *You gotta believe me, Mister!* This will be an enjoyable time for you. However, it is best to move on after he gets released. Being in jail has made a man out of him, something he is typically eager to showcase to Jody and Biff and the rest of the gang.

AMERICAN GARDEN HUMANS
IDENTIFICATION GUIDE

Male Common
Cackling Patch-Eye

Female Lesser
Garbled Broad

Male Pectoral
Surf Teen

PHONE-FACED BUSINESS TYCOON

This man—possibly due to the metal appendage on his face, no one knows for sure—is wary of a place called the Stock Market. He scowls when anyone mentions it. Outside of that, he reacts to barely anything. His call sounds like, *Get it done.* If you assist him in his problems shopping at the Stock Market, he is content to assist you in return. He will remain shy no matter how long he knows you, spending most of his time inside the limousine where he lives. The Phone-Faced Business Tycoon is sometimes female, it should be noted, and, in these cases, nothing will fall on the car and crush her.

PLAIN WHITE-COLLARED KNOW-IT-ALL

(also called the *Spectacled Smew*)

This man can be found on constant sabbatical from the university or hospital where he works. He will call it *sabbatical*, but it really will seem more like research leave. Distinguishing features include a coat that's not warm, in either tweed or white, that serves to advertise to other humans his availability as a Know-It-All. He can be found stroking his chin, walking from one indoor area to another, or writing in his journal. His call sounds like, *Let Me Show You Something!* He can also be identified by his habit of dragging a lady by the arm—any type of lady who's nearby. This man is not outwardly aggressive, but he is extremely boring, which may lull you into oblivion. In his own dull way, he is just as dangerous as the *Brooding Nighthawk*, the *Bare-bellied Midriff*, or the *American or European Bald Man*.

REGAL GREAT-CRESTED FIGHTER

This man speaks with a vague accent and he has elaborate headwear, which might include a vizier's headdress, a crown, a military beret, a Kaiser helmet, or the like. He is the leader of a large group that can offer any assistance you may need. His call sounds like *Unleash the beast!* However, if you opt to engage with this human, he will become more and more agitated over the course of the relationship, and while never a real threat to you, it might be easier just to eat him.

AMERICAN GARDEN HUMANS

— IDENTIFICATION GUIDE —

Male Ruff-Collared
Mullet

Female Stripe-Cheeked
Roadrunner

Female Yellow-Mouthed
Captivator

RUFF-COLLARED MULLET

This man is so eager to help you out of any jam that he'll speed through the countryside in a truck, kicking up a rather irritating dust cloud. He believes the two of you have in common an uncompromising drive to be wild and free, and thus he wants you to be the main attraction at his private zoo. He may hoot and wave a hat. Even raw, he tastes like fried chicken. (Sometimes also called the *American Whooping Coot*.)

STRIPE-CHEEKED ROADRUNNER

This lady's face features a prominent stripe, formed by a streak of grease or by a cut that never really bleeds. This stripe traces along her otherwise perfect and clean cheekbone. It will be clearly visible because this woman will typically stare back at you over her shoulder while she runs very fast in stiletto pumps. This woman may fall a few times, but she will still be faster than you are.

YELLOW-MOUTHED CAPTIVATOR

This lady has mustard in the corner of her mouth. In response, the *Brooding Nighthawk* typically cocks his head, reaches across the table of their booth at the diner, and dabs the mustard with a napkin. It should be noted that this will always be a small and adorable amount of mustard. If the woman's mouth is slathered in mustard, and it's coating her teeth, you are probably looking at a *Full-Throated or Large-Bellied Buffoon*. If this is, in fact, a *Yellow-Mouthed Captivator*, the Nighthawk's dabbing action will trigger a hormone surge in his body. He will become very territorial as far as she is concerned, and he may charge if you approach her.

An Illustration of Human
Inability to Share

APPENDIX III

Tables and Illustrations on the Human Temperament

Hyperbole

BLATANT, OBVIOUS EXAGGERATION is a distinguishing feature of the human temperament. It is known as *hyperbole*. This tendency to rely on overstatement is observable and consistent. What is unclear is the degree of intentionality that underlies it.

HYPERBOLE REGARDING TOOLS

AS DISCUSSED EARLIER, humans have not created their own tools for a long time. However, they frequently cite *skill with tools* as a distinctive trait of humanity.

The truth is that humans are not only divorced from the ability they had in the past to *make* tools, but they are largely inept at the *use* of tools. At no time is this more evident than when thousands of humans settle onto lounging surfaces in order to snack and to view other humans using wallpaper scrapers. However, even such highly skilled tool users as those on *home improvement shows* did not make the tools in use during these exhibitions.

In spite of the claim to be distinguishable from other species because of skill with tools, humans simultaneously understand that most primates use them. Stone hammers have been discovered—by humans—in the areas where chimpanzees live. Furthermore, a host of nonprimates are regularly observed making and using tools. Still, though, most humans maintain—and will argue until *closing time*—that they are unique in the creation and use of tools. It is possible that hyperbole is hardwired and instinctual.

TABLE 1 includes some common tools and examples of animals that use them. In some cases, these tools are simply found objects.

More often, though, the animals actually create or shape the items for their intended uses. For example, crows fashion hooks on their "fishing rods." Table 1 illustrates the extent of human *hyperbolic self-perception* regarding proficiency with tools.

Table 1: Non-Human Tool Usage, about Which Humans Are Aware and Somehow Also Not Aware

TOOL	SPECIES
Hammer	Chimpanzee, Otter, Wasp, Bear
Dental floss	Macaque
Whistle, Megaphone, Umbrella	Orangutan
Measuring stick	Gorilla
Protective "armor"	Octopus, Dolphin
Drain plug, flyswatter	Elephant
Lever	Cockatoo, Bonobo, Otter
"Fishing rod" to lure/ catch prey	Chimpanzee, Egyptian vulture, Striated heron
Hunting Spear	Chimpanzee

HYPERBOLE REGARDING LANGUAGE

IN ADDITION TO tool usage, humans consider their language skills unique. It is true that humans are excellent at the (human) languages they learn as juveniles, which perhaps makes them feel good about themselves. Positive emotions cause human brains to secrete serotonin, which could account for feelings of superiority. In that altered state, their own language seems as though it will be understandable to everyone if it is simply spoken *louder*.

TABLE 2 lists non-human species that have learned human languages, often quite rapidly and without much help. It also indicates whether the average human, conversely, has the aptitude to learn other species' means of communication. That is, are there humans "speaking" gorilla or, at the very least, conveying comprehension that gorillas can recognize? (Can humans ask a gorilla for a light, for example?)

Table 2: Potential for Random Individual to Comprehend Another Species' Vocalizations, Signs, Symbols, and/or Body Language

SPECIES	LIKELY	UNLIKELY
Gorilla	X	
Dolphin	X	
Dog	X	
Parrot	X	
Human		X

HYPERBOLE REGARDING SYMBOLS

IN WRITTEN TEXT, humans use exaggerated pictograms to represent their own countenances (see TABLE 3). When they type these symbols, typically while walking in traffic, their expressions are, in reality, entirely blank.

Table 3

EMOJI	ACTUAL FACE

HYPERBOLE IN NOISES

THE NOISES IN the speech balloons below are responses to stories others have shared, often related to minor problems about which the listener does not care.

HYPERBOLE IN SOCIAL BEHAVIOR

HUMANS PERCEIVE THEIR basic social unit as the monogamous pair. These couples, who mate for life, rear young together, and grow old together, are considered the bedrocks of human society. Statistically, however, fewer than 30 percent of adult humans worldwide actively engage in this coupling practice at any given time. Thus, comments such as *What are you doing with your life? Everyone else is married already!* should be understood as *hyperbole.* The word *everyone* = 100 percent. You can defuse potentially threatening situations by replicating the above human call. It has a documented demotivating effect, resulting in round-the-clock lounging and gaming.

HYPERBOLE IN "DEFENSIVE" BEHAVIOR

HUMANS OFTEN ENDEAVOR to hide aggressive intentions in order to strike their victims unawares. They camouflage animus even among themselves. Any combative human, whether the instigator of an argument about *those socks on the floor* or the aggressor in a *bar fight,* may engage in this behavior.

Often referred to hyperbolically as *being defensive*, the behavior is usually easy to identify because the human says, "I'm not defensive! You're defensive!" However, sometimes an aggressive statement can be further disguised because it is cunningly phrased as a question. Although easy to mistake for defensive or anti-predatory stances when taken at face value, the calls listed below exemplify aggressive *warning* behaviors, similar in threat level to growling or the baring of teeth:

- "Can you get off my case?"
- "Are you kidding me?"
- "What's your deal?"
- "Are we doing this?"
- "What's your problem?"

If humans add the phrase *right now* or *for real* to the above questions, this signifies even greater volatility. Here's the good news, though: a human generally follows such remarks with long and unbearable silence. Thus, you should have plenty of opportunity to eat, maul, or ward off aggressors before they become real threats to your safety. As the old show business adage says, timing is everything.

Acknowledgments

Many individuals possessed unsafe knowledge of this project. Some even dedicated energy to its completion, risking their well-being and reputations.

Thanks to the literary fiends who suffered rough drafts: Betsy Boyd, Elisabeth Dahl, Christine Grillo, Jen Grow, Elizabeth Hazen, Michael Kimball, James Magruder, Jen Michalski, Glen Retief, Gabriella Souza, Marion Winik. Thanks to James Tate Hill at Monkeybicycle for publishing an earlier incarnation of the mummy chapter, entitled "How to Survive a Human Attack: A Mummy's Decree (Papyrus Edition)," as well as editors at Defenestration for publishing "How to Survive a Human Attack: Swamp Monster Makeovers." Television titans Dan Vebber and Rich Dahm kindly offered advocacy at every stage. Human Attack Mediator Courtney Miller-Callihan of Handspun Literary Agency fought to get the guide into the right claws.

Many thanks to the Running Press team. Editor Jess Riordan took a chance on dicey work and facilitated a wholly/holy immersive monster experience. Designer Celeste Joyce brought lifelike luster to the distressed text. Proofreaders Diana Drew and Susan Hom ensured no fatal mistakes. Illustrator extraordinaire Joseph McDermott supercharged the visual story, animating the peril in ingenious and crafty ways. A quiet shout-out is due to Alina O'Donnell, Kara Thornton, and Amy Cianfrone for overtly, covertly getting the word out.

At home in the lair, Howard Yang served as Chief Preternatural Advisor, offering a depth of information about movie monsters that was disturbing. No matter the obstacle or foe, he maintained infectious enthusiasm that enlivened the project. Thanks to the brood for support—Mom, Kate, Monica, Steph, Zac, Rachelle, Sue, Nick, as well as the little monsters.

In loving memory of Dad, who enjoyed pondering the strange habits of humans along with a Manhattan on the rocks. Cheers.

About the Author

K.E. FLANN, PRETERNATURALIST

Renowned preternaturalist, K.E. Flann, holds PhD's in disciplines that include Covert Forestry, Urban Disorganization, Robust Outdoor Pursuits, Human Husbandry & Management, and Interdimensional Cooperation.

At the Ministry of Preternatural Resources, Flann serves as Cranial Impact Assessment Officer, drawing upon years of experience with paved areas, including Food Lion and the gas station, to ensure safe passage for visitors to the human world. During a distinguished career, Flann designed activities now accepted as best practice for introducing preternatural beings to their surroundings—these include human petting zoos, chasing demonstrations, and audio tours with rentable headsets.

The beautiful PreterNature Center is where Flann declines to answer questions from school children, the general population, or workers servicing the snack machines. With the exception of occasional guided public hikes to botanical landfills, during which visitors can collect parking fees, Flann maintains a general disconnect from human society. This lack of commitment provides the trustworthy voice on which supernatural, mutant, and AI beings have come to rely for objective guidance.

Inspired by Roman thinker, Juvenal, who famously said, "It is difficult not to write satire," Flann eschews difficulty by penning work for McSweeney's Internet Tendency, The Weekly Humorist, Points in Case, Frazzled, Greener Pastures, Monkeybicycle, and other publications.